From Stagecraft to Witchcraft

Patricia Crowther

By the same Author

The Witches Speak

Witch Blood!

The Secrets of Ancient Witchcraft

Witchcraft in Yorkshire

Witches Were For Hanging

Lid Off The Cauldron

The Zodiac Experience

One Witch's World
(Published in the U.S.A as High Priestess)

From Stagecraft
to Witchcraft

Patricia Crowther

Copyright © 2020   Fenix Flames Publishing Ltd   Patricia Crowther

All rights reserved including the right of reproduction in whole or in part in any form. No reporduction, copy or transmission of this publication may be made without written permission. No paragraph of this publication may be reproduced, copied or transmitted save with written permission or in accordance with the provisions of the Copyright Act 1956 (as amended). Any person who performs any unauthorised act in relation to this publication may be liable to criminal prosecution and civil claims for damages. The moral rights of the author have been asserted.

First published 2002
This edition first published 2020

Design & Layout:
Sarah Kay / Ashley Mortimer / Fenix Flames Publishing Ltd

Cover photograph: Gwion; all other photographs supplied by Patricia Crowther.

Printed by Lightning Source International/Ingram Spark
Published by Fenix Flames Publishing Ltd

ISBN   978-1-913768-03-4

About the Author

Patricia Crowther, a native of Yorkshire, has been a practising witch since 1960, when she was initiated into the Craft by Gerald Brosseau Gardner. A High Priestess of the Great Goddess, she is now recognised as a Grand Mother of the Craft. Patricia is also heir to an hereditary tradition passed on to her in 1962 by an elderly Scottish High Priestess. As a doyenne of the Old Religion, she is a leading and respected spokesperson and has lectured widely, both in this country and abroad. She has regularly appeared on television and radio, and written many books on the subject, including Lid off the Cauldron. Her autobiography, One Witch's World was published by Robert Hale Ltd. In her spare time, she studies astrology, promotes animal welfare, and dotes on her beloved cat, Sheba.

In Memory of

Sarah Louise Kay

9th April 1992 - 5th January 2019

Contents

1 Made in Sheffield 11

2 The Smell of the Greasepaint 65

3 Romance & Rodents 93

4 "Who is Arnold Crowther?" 114

5 A Magical World 146

Prayer To The Goddess 178

The Jean MacDonald Letters 179

Chapter 1
Made in Sheffield

Like many people born in Sheffield, I am proud of my roots and fiercely defend the city in which I was born. My parents, Clare and Alfred Dawson, ran four tobacconist and sweet shops in Sheffield when I made my appearance, and they lived on the premises of one shop in Duke Street.

I was born half-an-hour into the 14th October on a stormy night, a phenomenon which coincided with my difficult birth. This had been predicted by a local palmist, but she also said that both my mother and I would survive the ordeal.

Apart from coming into the world when the wind was howling round the house and the rain lashed against the window-panes, there was nothing to suggest that I would eventually become known as 'The Sheffield Witch', although my great grandmother had been a practising wise-woman in Brittany before she came to Sheffield. She met and married one William Dawson who hailed from Dublin, so there is a mixture of French, Irish and English in my blood.

Miranda, my grandmother on my mother's side, died in her forties (long before I was born) having given birth to ten children. Mother said she was very lovely, her dark hair framing delicate features and the most startling blue eyes. Miranda had a sister whose name was Caroline Trevelyan-Corker-Goddard-Grant. She was known as 'Trevy', for short!

Trevy had married a Cornish man, and when my mother visited their cottage in Normanton Spring near Woodhouse, she often mentioned that things were different there, because Trevy had lots of herbs about the place and often looked into the future through a dark-blue glass ball.

1. My parents, Alfred and Clare Dawson

I was so protected in my early years that I contracted almost every common ailment, available, including an abscess on my neck as large as a tea-cup. The excellent Dr. Callaghan lanced it to my tearful whispers of, "Oh thank you. Thank you". Both Dr. Callaghan, and his successor, Dr. Billington, worked overtime on me!

Dr. Callaghan's premises were opposite my parent's shop in Duke Street and his ten year old son would come into the shop and demand a ha'porth of shag (loose tobacco). My mother, being grateful to his father, would say. "You are under age young man", then serve him quickly, telling him to hide it away.

We had a wire-haired fox terrier called Tony, who was older than me, and he would pick a fight with any other dog in sight, if none were to be seen, he would go and find one. He also hated people in uniform or anyone whom he considered alien to his territory. Tony was the terror of Duke Street but he was a very good guard dog.

A neighbour would scream, "Oh, 'e's got me cat!", while Tony walked proudly round the yard with the unfortunate animal dangling from his jaws. Mother would hasten to reassure the woman that Tony would not hurt it, and indeed, he did not. After a few perambulations of his patch, to show who was boss, he would release the cat, unharmed.

My little cousin, Alwyn, spent time with us, and one day he crawled under the table and sat down next to Tony. He intended to copy Tony's actions, but as the dog was merely sitting down, there was not much Alwyn could do except sit beside him.

2. One of my parents' tobacconist's shops, Lady's Bridge, Sheffield.
The lady assistant was with us for many years.

Tony was not amused at this and bared his teeth, growling menacingly. To my horror, Alwyn did the same, putting his face close to Tony's. I expected him to be bitten at any moment. I think I must have screamed, because my mother rushed in, and following my pointing finger, ordered Alwyn to stop the game, immediately.

Tony was fierce courageous dog. He only bit me once, and it was my own fault as I was teasing him at the time. Having the wound cauterized at the local chemist's taught me never to tease an animal, again.

The row of shops where we lived contained a butcher's shop and I heard awful stories of how he caught rats and scalded them to death in a tub. He owned a bull mastiff and one day it chased me until fell, screaming with fear. I was always falling down and often wonder how I succeeded as a dancer.

A succession of servants took me out twice a day, in my perambulator. Close by, there was Norfolk Park and the Cholera Grounds, the latter contained a tall monument erected over a mass grave of people who had died from the disease in the 1800's. Despite this, it was a pleasant place with well-kept flower beds and lawns and a view over the city.

My parents had a lot of trouble with the girls they employed as shop assistants. Quite a number of them stole money and goods and were summarily dismissed. One girl had stuffed her shoes with notes and hidden gold and silver cigarette cases in her bedroom. In my mind's eye I can still see one of the culprits weeping at the door, her suitcase at her feet. The police were not informed of these crimes, as my parents believed that by losing their employment, the girls had been punished enough.

It was discovered that one girl was pregnant, so her father was asked to come and collect her. She was terrified of him and said he would probably kill her if he found out about her condition.

So, when her father knocked on the front door, she departed via the door at the back. It was a close run thing.

My mother was extremely independent and at the age of seventeen, in order to start up in business, she borrowed five hundred pounds from her great-aunt - a large sum in those days. My parents, who were engaged to be married at the time, rented a fruit shop in Duke Street and worked hard to repay the loan and buy furniture for when they married.

Every evening, before closing the shop, they covered the fruit and vegetables, displayed in the window, with white sheets, and one night, a policeman on his beat was amazed to see the sheets undulating in the light of his torch. It turned out to be rats, busily gnawing their way through the produce. They took bites out of all the fruit, including every single grape!

The floor and walls of the shop were duly sealed, but noises came from a potato bin. When it was raised, a rat appeared with an injured leg. It hobbled out of the shop and up the street where it surprised an old tabby cat dozing in the sun. As the rat limped past, the cat did a double take, then pounced.

Prior to our dog Tony's arrival, or even mine, my parents doted upon a rough-haired fox terrier called, Floss. This much-loved animal had a yen for peas, and would carry a few pods from the shop into the middle of Duke Street, where tram-cars ran up and down all the time. Oblivious of any danger, Floss would sit down and proceed to open the pods and consume their contents. Tram-drivers would swear and slam on their brakes; at the same time producing a hissing noise from the vehicle in order to make Floss move out of the way. Many of these drivers would try to avoid being put on that particular route because of "That damned dog!"

Floss became very ill and my parents called in the vet; and cancelled a holiday in order to nurse her. However, she passed away, and with many tears, was buried in my Aunt Annie's garden at Crookes, a garden which at that time, overlooked one of Sheffield's reservoirs. A large, framed picture of Floss remains to this day with the caption, "Our Floss, loved".

3. Beloved Floss who had a penchant for peas

4. Little thing walking in the Cholera Grounds, Norfolk Road, Sheffield

After their marriage, my parents moved into the tobacconist's shop a few doors further down Duke Street, and one night were awakened by the ghostly sounds of the piano being played, downstairs. When my father went to investigate, it turned out to be a rat which had got into the back of the instrument and was striking the wires as it moved around. The creature was persuaded to abandon its musical endeavours and escaped when my Father opened the back door. All the shops in Duke Street were old properties and rats were prevalent, but I'm happy to say that the 'musical rat' was the last one to trouble my parents.

While on the subject of rats, I must mention an extraordinary happening that that occurred in Sheffield in the early 1990's. Some building work was in progress near the River Don, and one night hundreds of rats came out of that river and with the king rat leading them, moved en masse through the city, keeping to the main thoroughfares. They were seen by policemen on night duty, who observed the phenomena in awestruck silence. The rats moved like a huge black shadow through the empty streets and upon reaching the river Sheaf on the other side of the city, they disappeared between its banks.

My mother's beautiful, younger sister, Minnie, had what was called, fluid round the heart - a form of dropsy, and the doctor said, "If you gave me enough gold to line the streets, I could not save her."

Months after Minnie's death, my mother went into the shop to look for something. It was nearly dark, but she knew her way around so did not switch on the lights. As she bent down under the counter, she heard a rustling sound behind her. Looking round, she saw a white swathed figure in the corner surrounded by a bluish-white light. "Oh God Min!" she gasped, staring at the apparition, unable to move. The features of the wraith were covered, but she knew who it was. When the vision vanished, mother stumbled into the living-room convinced she had seen the shade of her dead sister.

5. Sitting on my father's knees in Norfolk Park, with Aunt Annie (left) and cousin Deidre.

When my father came home she was still upset and trembling and he commented, "Well, dear, Minnie does not want you to forget her, that's all." Mother was expecting me at the time, so naturally her thoughts were centred upon the coming baby. However, the anniversary of her sister's death was only two days away and mother said, "You must put her memorium in the paper first thing in the morning." A request that was duly carried out.

I attended the Norfolk Kindergarten and eventually enjoyed learning my lessons. I noticed that one of the little chairs had a white patch on the seat, and if at all possible, the children would avoid sitting on that one. One little girl wet her knickers, regularly, and was nearly always obliged to sit on 'her' chair.

In the annual nativity play I was chosen to be an Eskimo, covered from head to toe in a white, woolly garment, and I so wanted to be one of the angels! I thought it strange that a plump, dark-haired girl played one of the angels, when she would have made an ideal Eskimo, but I had to grin and bear it.

Mary Henstock, the Principal's daughter, always had the best parts in plays and pageants, so of course she was 'Mary' in the nativity play. I learned from a very early age that it is not always what you can do, but *who you know* that governs how you get on in life.

Most of the children had lunch at school and Mary and me would save our desserts (which usually took the form of jelly-based puddings) and take them up to the bathroom. Mary would then introduce some Andrews Liver Salts into the puddings, producing what can best be described as a revolting, gooey mess, which we spooned eagerly into our mouths. I cannot remember any adverse effects from all this, but then, I was always horribly constipated, anyway. I was made to sit upon my potty for hours, or so it seemed, with no end result, and had to be dosed every day with syrup of figs.

6. The nativity play at Norfolk Kindergarten. Self on the left as an Eskimo.

One day, we were taken into the Vicarage garden to watch Queen Mary pass by in her car. Many years later, I saw her again in London entering a theatre in Drury Lane. We both looked much older!

My god-parents, Ben and Edie Riley kept the 'Brown Bear' hotel in Norfolk Street, Sheffield. Uncle Ben (as I was told to call him), was a six-foot, handsome, jolly man who sported a white suit and a car to match. He caused quite a stir in the neighbourhood when he appeared.

Uncle Ben bought me marvellous toys and would seize me and lift me high above his head - sometimes tossing me into the air. I was always terrified of this, and when he arrived I would try to catch hold of the furniture in order to stop it happening, but it never did.

I liked him, and his presents, but dreaded his inevitable welcome, usually accompanied by the words, "And how is my little princess, today?" His 'little princess' was feeling distinctly sick and in danger of throwing-up all over his lovely white suit! Luckily, this never actually occurred.

Ben and Edie bought me a carved wood, pull-away circus. All the animals, including the ring-master, could be pulled apart, and the arms and legs, rearranged to make fabulous monsters. It was a lovely gift and I still have three of the animals to this day. Another present was a child's tea-set in bone china with the coat-of-arms of the Isle of Man set upon each piece. It may have been a portent of the future, as many years later, my initiation into witchcraft took place on that very island.

My mother, Clare Dawson, was one of the first women in Sheffield to sport the Eton Crop hair-style. This involved having her lovely long auburn hair lopped off to mimic the Eton school-boys very short hair-cut. Once, I peeked into a drawer and saw her tresses laid there in tissue paper. I was pleased when hairstyles changed again and my mother's hair once more grew thick and luxuriant.

Among my parents' friends were the Robinson's, whose daughters, Phyllis and Iris toured the world with their vocal act. Phyllis Robins (her stage name), became a singer with Henry Hall's famous orchestra. His late night radio programmes and his familiar voice, saying, "This is Henry Hall speaking", could not be missed. Radio was in its infancy and an enthralling wonder of the times.

Phyllis, with such numbers as "I've got a dog, he's lost in the fog. Will some kind gentleman see me home?", recorded vocals with many well-known orchestras of those days. I was taken back-stage at the Empire Theatre in Sheffield to see Phyllis Robins - a vision of loveliness in an exquisite pink gown - and she presented me with a photograph, signed, "With love to Pat, from Auntie Phyllis, 1934."

The mother of Ben Warriss (one half of the famous comedy duo, Jewel and Warriss), was a member of the Builders Exchange Club in Sheffield, and a friend of my parents, who were also members of it. Jimmy and Ben were cousins, born in Sheffield, and also in the same bed - though not at the same time. We went to see them in pantomime at the Empire Theatre with a friend and her daughter, Anne, and I fell in love with Jimmy Jewel, there and then! We sat in a box near the stage and felt very grand.

One day, Anne and her mother came to see us before another visit to the theatre, and I asked, "Are you going to sit in a box?" Little Anne tossed her head and piped up, "We *always* sit in a box!" whereupon everyone laughed, and her words became a catch-phrase of ours ever after.

7. An apprehensive "Fairy on the Moon" at the Builders Exchange Club's Christmas Party 1931

Because I was so terribly shy my mother took me to the Constance Grant Academy of Dance, the most prestigious in Sheffield at that time. Miss Grant had grave doubts about my being able to perform a solo, due to my nervousness, but my mother was adamant that I be taught one. And as I had at least three lessons at the Academy every week, my teacher graciously acquiesced.

I was taught a song and dance number entitled, "So Shy", which just happened to be a popular song of the day. Miss Grant's mother, a French lady, was an expert dressmaker and created the first of many subsequent costumes for me. It consisted of a flame-coloured georgette blouse and silver lame trousers with georgette gussets. A floppy-brimmed hat of similar materials completed the outfit.

The Academy was to hold a matinee at the Sheffield Empire Theatre which was to include my stage debut. When the time came, I stood in the wings with mother, trembling violently and wanting to be sick. Then I heard my music being played by the orchestra, and as I stepped onto the stage I was suddenly filled with a strange elation. The stage seemed vast, and the blazing spotlights mercifully hid the sea of faces - I saw only darkness beyond them. I finished to a roar of applause and was sent back to take a curtain call. Miss Grant said, "Well, I'm blest", or words to that effect! Someone from the Jack Buchanan show, featured at the Empire that week, remarked, "She should go to London, to the Royal Academy of Dramatic Art, to be trained for the theatre", but such a thing was not possible at that time.

I had short, thick, fair hair which was put into rags every night to make it curl. The hair was wound onto strips of linen - each one tied into a knot. That's why it was called 'rags'.

8. My dancing teacher Constance Grant, on the occasion of her marriage to the musician Harry Sylvester.

9. The photograph 'Auntie' Phyllis Robins gave me when she appeared at the Empire Theatre, Sheffield, in 1934.

Miss Grant became more enthusiastic about me and thought up a new idea for a ballet dance. I was to be 'Bubbles' after the famous painting by Millais. Dressed like the boy in the picture, I wore the green velvet tunic with the white frilled collar. My hair was already like his, so that was no problem. A large, gilt frame was made, and when the curtain went up I was sitting inside it holding a bowl and a white, long-stemmed pipe, looking up in wonder at the 'bubble' I had blown. At the end of my dance, I returned to the frame, and again took up the pose.

With this dance, I won the highest marks in the International Dancing Masters Association competition at Blackpool, receiving a gold medal, a certificate, and the coveted silver Rose Bowl. The winner could hold it for nine months, and their name was engraved on a shield at its base.

Out of five hundred competitors from all parts of the British Isles, whose ages ranged from six to eighteen years, I had gained 95 marks out of a possible hundred throughout all the age sections.

A photograph of my 'Bubbles' appeared in the *Daily Mirror* and other newspapers. It was my first glimpse of success! Incidentally, Eric Morley, the producer of 'Miss World' the international beauty competition, was one of the officials at Blackpool.

In my second year at Blackpool I gained the highest marks yet again! This time, however, I tied with Constance Grant's assistant teacher, Emily Chadburn, so we walked across the dance floor side by side to receive the Rose Bowl. It must have been a bit awkward for Emily, sharing the bowl with a mite like me from the 'Baby Section', although it was another honour for Constance Grant's academy. Both our names were engraved upon the trophy (mine for a second time!), and we shared the nine months that we held it.

10. "Bubbles" , (after the famous painting by Millais) with the Blackpool Rose Bowl. 1933

11. With some of my medals and trophies, including the coveted 'Rose Bowl'.

They say the third time pays for all, and it certainly did for me! The third year at Blackpool was unlucky - for me at least. During my musical-comedy number, "Pennies from Heaven", I missed out the most important part of my dance. This had something to do with the music being repeated at one stage. It was an expensive error. Awarded 95 marks, I lost the Rose Bowl by only one mark, as I failed to perform for the required time. The adjudicators gave that crucial mark of 96 to Hazel Honey (also from Sheffield), who, for the record, danced to the same music.

Much was the chagrin, the weeping and the tearing of hair. The hat trick, of winning three times, consecutively, when I would have kept the Rose Bowl for good, was not to be. My mother was furious with me for forgetting part of my dance, and Hazel Honey's mother, a satisfied smirk on her face, commented, "Oh don't be cross with Patricia. I'm sure she did her best." A remark which did nothing to improve the situation, as you may imagine. I was extremely upset, but at least I came second, with a silver medal and a certificate, but it seemed to count for nothing at the time.

A group of dancers, including myself, were taught a character dance entitled, 'Child Immortal", in which I took the part of a ghost child who came to play with the living children. I was distinguished as the phantom by wearing a white floaty dress, while the other dancers wore blue. The audience was visibly moved to tears at the end, when the children went away and left me alone.

A solo dance was adapted from Hans Christian Anderson's "The Little Match Girl", who sees wonderful visions when she strikes her last three matches. In the light of the final one she sees her grandmother who carries her off to heaven. Another weepy!

12. Holding the first prize for the character dance, 'Teasing', Blackpool 1935. That year, small cups replaced the customary medals.

13. In a variety show at the Victoria Hall in Sheffield, featuring a song and dance number."F. D. R. Jones" with chorus and babes.

My parents sold the shops and became proprietors of a hotel, "Ye Olde Harrow Inn", in Broad Street, Sheffield. After a time, however, they moved again, to the "Noah's Ark", another watering-hole in a less populated area at Intake. They believed it would be more healthy for us all, but in fact it was quite the reverse.

I was sent to a council school in Mansfield Road, which I hated. There were so many children - so many rough boys, that I dreaded walking through the gates. Then, children started coming to school with their throats wrapped up, and I contracted diphtheria and nearly died. The swab taken from my throat was somehow delayed and precious time was lost in the diagnosis of the disease. Late one night, I was wrapped in blankets and carried into a waiting ambulance. I felt very ill and could hardly swallow but I noticed that the interior of the ambulance had gleaming silvery panels.

At Lodge Moor hospital, white-coated doctors laid me naked upon a table, examining my throat and other parts of my anatomy and discussing my chances, *sotto voce*. They gave me eight injections, then I was again wrapped in blankets and deposited in a large ward with hot water-bottles packed tightly around me. I was soon trembling and shivering as the drugs commenced fighting the disease, and a nurse brought me the most deliciously cool orange drink - it tasted wonderful. I did not remember much after that as I was unconscious for a week, except for a few lucid moments when I was aroused for bodily functions and more of that lovely drink.

I could not use a bed-pan properly, and every time I was given one, I wet the bed. The sheets had to be changed at least twice a day. This incurred the wrath of the Sister, who marched up and gave me a lecture, pointing to a girl in the next bed and praising her for her competent use of the utensil. The Sister's face turned to jelly as I again lapsed into unconsciousness. I entered a dream world where all the beds in the ward folded themselves up against the wall, including the one next to mine!

My parents were only allowed to see me through the window, and one day when my mother visited me, she found that my bed was empty. She stared through the glass, unable to move, then a nurse ran up and told her not to worry. I had developed a rash which they thought might be scarlet fever and I had been taken to the Observation Ward in another block. I had regained my senses, and while being wheeled through the corridors, I pleaded with them to tell my parents where I had gone, I was filled with terror in case, they would not be able to find me.

The rash turned out to be due to the drugs, but it had helped me to gain more salubrious surroundings. This new ward was made almost entirely of huge windows and each patient had their own private room. The sun shone into the building and outside I could see trees and flowers.

My mother visited me more than my father as he had to hold the fort in her absence. I smiled at her through the glass. She always had a lovely bright scarf on her shoulders and I always asked her for it. Soon, I had quite a collection of them, little knowing that whatever entered my room would be burned when I had gone. Unfortunately, this included a favourite toy cat of mine - a grey, long-haired beauty with green eyes, that I had asked for.

In the previous ward, enemas had been regularly administered; a hateful feeling of being filled up inside with cold water. The water must have been heated, somewhat, but it always felt icy-cold. Now I was left to my own devices which resulted in a big 'nothing doing'. So, I was given a suppository, which only produced great pain. Another was supplied, and I realised that faith would indeed have to move mountains, as the nurse kept her eye on me through an internal window. After about ten minutes or more, she looked questioningly at me and foolishly I nodded my head when I should have given negative signal "Fool", I thought, and there ensued a mighty battle, which because I was so weak, nearly finished me off. I struggled and fought from my difficult supine position, and attempted to improve it by supporting my body on my elbows, but even that small action, failed.

I know that the nurse would appear at any moment, and if despite the agony, renewed my efforts. At last, I won, my bedclothes bathed in perspiration. My relief was enormous but I could not relax upon my pillows until everything was tidied up. The features of the nurse registered disbelief as she took the utensil away, and I chuckled weakly to myself. In spite of this latest trial I was beginning to feel a little better.

When I was allowed out of bed, my legs would not work properly, so the ward Sister supported me and walked me up and down the verandah. She was a jolly, Scottish lady, and a big improvement on the previous Sister. She held on to me, as my legs refused to support me, and this went on for many days. In some cases of diphtheria, it attacks the muscles, and paralysis ensues, but luckily, my limbs at last began to obey the commands of my brain, and I slowly started to walk again.

The day I left hospital was a joyous one, indeed. It was full of happy surprises. When I walked into my bedroom, I discovered a brand new bedroom suite - a present from my parents. The dressing-table was full of pink flowers, reflected in the three mirrors which immediately caught my eye. I was suddenly interested in my own reflection -I was growing up!

My father gave me two new books, *A Book of Old Ballads* filled with legends of heroes, and *A Masque of May Morning*, which, as the title suggests, was a play, but a play with a difference. All the characters were flowers and the story revolved around the May Queen.

I realised at this time, that my dear father's health was not good. During the first World War he had been exempt from call-up into the forces because he made surgical instruments. All grinders were weakened by the dust from the grinding-stones, as it settled on their lungs. No man in that kind of work anticipated a long life.

It was decided that we could all do with a holiday, so someone was found to run the hotel in my parent's absence, and off we went to Southery in Lincolnshire. My father wanted to try his hand at fishing and this tiny hamlet had been recommended, where fishing took place. (!)

The local hostelry was in the form of a thatched cottage, where beer was served from a large cask on the kitchen table. When we arrived, we were taken to a ladder which led upstairs! Having negotiated this primitive appliance, we found the bedroom under the eaves. It was quite pretty, with a double and a single bed, and when we retired for the night, an oil lamp was lit, which made everything look very cosy.

In the night, we were awakened by the sound of footsteps upon the ladder, and a dark figure appeared. It walked through the bedroom and opened a door which must have led into another room. We had not been warned that this would happen! In the early morning light there was a repeat performance when the man vacated his room and I hid under the bedclothes.

Ablutions were performed by way of a jug of hot water and a basin. The necessary third item of the trio being located under the bed!

14. The 'Noah's Ark' Hotel, Intake, Sheffield, where the fire took place.

Father caught a large eel, then carefully put it back into the river, and if nothing else, we enjoyed the country air and the piquant accommodation.

Looking back, I think how strange it was to have lived in a hotel called "Noah's Ark", because originally it was Nuah's Ark, Nuah being an ancient name for the Great Goddess in Syria. The shape of an ark, is the vesica pisces, or feminine oval. Through the Goddess, all things are born!

While we were living there, a servant accidentally started a fire in the newly decorated kitchen, and I awoke in the early hours to find my bedroom full of smoke - I could see nothing but a thick, grey pall. Choking and coughing, I found my way to my parents' room and roused them. Had I not woken, we would all have died in our sleep.

The Fire Service was called and we escaped via an outside staircase. This, led off from a large room at the end of the building and had once been used by the 'Buffs' - members of the Royal Ancient Antideluvian Order of Buffaloes, a secret society. A door which connected the room with the upper floor had a secret panel in it, so that only initiates could enter.

When I was quite well again, I attended Eastbank High School, a private establishment where I was very happy. And due to my father's deteriorating health, we moved into a semidetached house in City Road. The other half of the semi was a funeral director's, and we were three doors away from City Road cemetery.

From my new bedroom, I had (and still have), a lovely view of the trees and greenery in the cemetery, and of course, our garden. There were no graves to be seen, not that it would have worried me unduly if any had been in view. The trees revealed the changing seasons, and the bare, black branches outlined against the pale pink eastern sky of a winter's dawn, were quite exquisite. Moving house was a temporary measure: "just for a few months", my parents said, but Fate decreed otherwise.

I had some imaginary Fairy friends in the new house, though they were very real to me. My favourite fairy was violet, and she was my confidante. When I helped my mother to dust, she always accompanied me from room to room, and with her help the work was done in no time. I had never seen a stately home at that time, yet for some reason I would call my bedroom 'the east wing' and my parents' room,' the west wing', and imagine myself as a maid employed in a big house.

It was decided that I was 'growing past my strength' I whatever *that* meant) and must have a rest from dancing for a while. Instead, I studied singing under Greta Rawson, a pupil of the famous soprano, Isobel Haillie, and voice production with two separate teachers, Lillias Hawson and Joyce Elshaw.

Joyce was a large, auburn-haired, jolly person with a wonderful soprano voice. She taught me a monologue called, "Helen sees a Ghost", which ended with a terrified scream. I was rather good at that!

World War 2 broke out, but for the time being, life went on as usual. During playtime at school. I would recruit as many children as possible to join me in singing various songs, and conducted them in such numbers as "South of the Border" - a particular favourite of mine. I was very cross when some of the children deserted me to continue with their games. One of them was John Billington, our doctor's son. He had red hair and a temper to match, and scowled, horribly, when asked to join in the singing.

I decided to put on a concert in the back-yard of my friend's house. Pauline Percival lived two doors away. It was to be a benefit concert for the Cot Fund of a local hospital and was organised by "Uncle Timothy" of the *Sheffield Star* newspaper. We sold tickets in the neighbourhood.

The first half of the programme consisted of songs, dances and monologues, and the second half featured a play, "*The Swineherd*", by Hans Christian Anderson. We rehearsed for weeks on end, mostly because Pauline and I enjoyed rehearsing, and we planned to use the newly-installed Anderson Shelter as a dressing-room.

These Government shelters were erected outside for when the Germans started to bomb us. Pauline's house belonged to the Sheffield Council, and these type of homes were the first ones to be thus supplied. Our own shelter was not installed until much later, when the bombing had already begun. We thought it was very apt to be performing a play by Hans Anderson and using an Anderson shelter in the process.

At the eleventh hour we had a refusal from Jean Taylor, who had a part in the play, and as producer/director I tore out my hair. Then, Pauline suggested Maureen Peck, who incidentally, had been the 'good' girl in the bed next to mine at the hospital. Maureen agreed to take part, and Pauline got her into the costume. Luckily, the lines she had to speak were few. I took the title role of the Swineherd, and Pauline played the Princess. The costumes were nice as we made use of my old ones which had been professionally made.

About thirty people came to see the show and all the children remembered their lines. We made two pounds, four shillings and eight pence, which was duly forwarded to "Uncle Timothy". He thanked us all and put our names in his newspaper column.

Lillias Hawson was asked to entertain the forces, stationed within a certain radius of the city, by putting on plays. I had small parts in two of them, "March Wedding" and 'Amazons on Broadway", and accompanied by my mother, we visited gun-sites, and army and air-force bases.

15. Demonstrating new steps to the troops, with ballroom teacher Sydney Grayson at Croft House Settlement.

I became a member of the Voluntary Entertainment Service and received a badge in the form of a white rose (for Yorkshire), inscribed with the words, 'V.E.S. Northern Command', which I wore with great pride. V.E.S. was a smaller division of the Entertainers National Services Association, or E.N.S.A., known to the troops as "Every night something awful".

At a regular pick-up point in the city, we would board a bus which had its windows blacked-out, so we had no idea of our destination. The canteens were always packed with servicemen, and one night a young lady played an accordion. That was it! I demanded to learn this instrument, and in due course obtained one and studied for three years with Charles Beldan Haigh, a professor of music. I later took piano lessons, too.

In order to earn a little money, I joined a dance band and received ten shillings a night. The dances were held every weekend at St. Swithun's Church Hall on the Manor Estate. I also played with Percy's Old Tyme band, too.

Playing with professional musicians taught me a lot about tempo, and I thoroughly enjoyed my work. Mother helped me to carry the accordion, which was 120 bass and quite heavy. Young men bound for the dance hall would offer to carry it for us, but soon put it down with a muttered excuse. We got quite used to all this, and when someone approached to help would look knowingly at each other. One chap exclaimed, "What have you got in there - pig iron?" But really, the instrument was quite easy to carry between us.

16. Walter Chappell's Accordion Band at the Regent Cinema, Barker's Pool (later called the Gaumont Cinema). Self, seated on right.

A young man at the dances would come up on stage and sing through the microphone. Gordon Gibson had a lovely voice and crooned just like Bing Crosby. He was also blonde and handsome, and always wore a smart grey suit. All the girls were in love with him. He usually danced with his girl-friend,

Doreen, a plump, dark-haired lady who always clutched a handkerchief in her hand, as though she expected to burst into tears at any moment. Everyone was jealous of Doreen, as Gordon whirled her round the floor. He kissed me, once, behind the curtains, and I was really thrilled. It was our secret. I sang, too, and one evening, Gordon and I sang a duet. I walked on air!

One day, he knocked on our door, his face streaming with blood. He had fallen off his bike, just outside our house. My mother tended his wounds but I could tell that she was glad when he had gone. Gordon was my first tiny heart-throb.

Many years later, I met Gordon again, while out shopping. A lady and two small children were trailing behind him. I was shocked at the change in him, he looked so tired and careworn. However, the lady was not Doreen. Perhaps she was at home crying into that handkerchief? I had yet to learn about the vagaries of love.

Another young man to whom I was attracted, was Ray Rawson who played the xylophone. We met at local concerts and one of them took place at the Victoria Hall in Norfolk Street. It was presented by English Steels for Aid to Russia, and awkwardly called, "Russiaing to Revue".

The show included the Sheffield Municipal Orchestra (officers guild) who were seated in tiers at the back of the stage. Their pianist was my teacher, Charles Haigh, and as this was my solo debut with the accordion, I was terrified, not least because my teacher was present. I was also very conscious of the experienced musicians sitting behind me as I stumbled through my selection. I thought I was terrible and was probably not the only one!

At my next lesson I was given the verdict, "Not bad. But why on earth did you attempt such advanced pieces? There are plenty of simpler ones you could have played - and more skillfully, too." Of course, he was absolutely right.

17. On stage at Collins Music Hall in London.

Ray Rawson sometimes called to see me, and he, too, was fair-haired and good-looking. One day, as he was leaving our house it started to rain, so, holding an umbrella, I accompanied him to the tram-stop which was just outside. Faster than Concorde, my mother appeared and hauled both me and the umbrella back into the house. It was most humiliating.

I know it was all done for the best of intentions, as both my parents wanted me to make something of myself and not be saddled with a husband and little ones, before I had time to think of a career. They were so wise in this as I also discovered, through my years as a teenager, how much you change and develop, and more particularly, how one's taste in the opposite sex matures, too.

There was talk of putting on a pantomime and Joyce Elshaw chose me to play the part of 'Maid Marion' with Ray as 'Robin Hood. I quite enjoyed rehearsing as there was a scene in which 'Robin' and 'Marion', kissed. But that did it. There were no more rehearsals after that and I never saw Ray, again.

I took part in the 'City of Sheffield Centenary of Incorporation Pageant', presented at the City Hall on Tuesday 24th August 1943. It was devised and written by the eminent L. du Garde Peach and produced by Laurie Lingard. The cast was prodigious and supplemented by many different services from Sheffield including the Women's Land Army, the Air Training Corps, and the Civil Defence. There were also detachments from the Police; the British Red Cross Society; members of Sheffield Philharmonic and Victoria Hall Choral Societies, and many others.

The pageant began with 'The First Charter', when Thomas Lord de Furnival granted the First Charter to Sheffield in 1297.

"To all free Tenants of this Town and their heirs, to hold in fee and heredity, freely, quietly, well, and in peace, for ever."

As its conclusion, there was a speech by the First Lord of the Admiralty, the Rt. Hon. A.V. Alexander, C.H., M.P.

I was chosen to be one of the two attendants to Mary, Queen of Scots, who was historically linked to Sheffield. The part of 'Mary' being played by Ella Atkinson, a well-known local actress.

Incidentally, in recent times there is often mention of the Scottish Queen being incarcerated in what is wrongly described as the 'Manor Castle'. In fact, for seven years she was kept in the Turret House in the grounds of Sheffield Manor House, under the guardianship of the Earl of Shrewsbury.

The gown and flowing headdress I wore in the Pageant were quite lovely, and one day the press arrived and we went outside for photographs to be taken. I thought I could feel a draught, and when I examined my dress I found that I had stepped into it the wrong way, so that most of the material was at the front. A mere flap of it at the back covered my confusion! It was a windy day, too, so my *derriere* was constantly exposed to all and sundry. My face was not the only part of me to look red!

I joined Walter Chappell's Ladies Accordion Band, where we wore white blouses, black skirts, and silly little page-boy hats.

I found it difficult at first, being 'third' accordionist, as this position entailed playing the harmony, rather than the actual melody.

The band was booked for a Sunday night concert at the Regent Cinema in Barker's Pool (later called the Gaumont Cinema). Jewel and Warriss, and other big names, including Ted and Barbara Andrews (the parents of the famous film star, Julie Andrews), also appeared. Stepping into the blazing spotlights, I sang "Mary's a Grand Old Name", with the band. This was another new role for me.

Soon afterwards, I was asked to give my services in a charity concert at Dial House Social Club. This was one of the largest clubs in Sheffield, and that night it was packed to the ceiling. I had never been in a club before, and when I saw a room the size of an aircraft hanger, with hundreds of people sitting round tables, I started to tremble. When not actually performing on stage, I was still self-conscious and shy, and the awful thing was that you had to walk through all people in order to gain the dressing-room. I sang, "Bless this House"; played the accordion, and received a ripple of applause. I was very relieved to breathe the night air, again.

The father of one of the artistes on the bill that night, asked me to join a concert party he ran, and suggested that when singing, I should accompany myself on the accordion. He also pointed out that if I worked the club circuit I should use another name. So as I already featured songs made famous by Bing Crosby, it was decided that 'Pat Crosby' would be suitable. Very gradually, I started to obtain bookings in some of the smaller clubs, and my voice continued to improve.

The high school I attended, closed, and it was thought advantageous for me to learn shorthand and typing, as show business can be a precarious profession. Whiteley's College on Surrey Street was selected, but due to being younger than the age stipulated for entry to this establishment, I took a preliminary examination, which I duly passed. And during the time I attended the college, I gained certificates in Intermediate and Advanced shorthand (the Pitman variety), and also in speed typing. In the event, I did not have to call upon these abilities to earn my bread, but the typing was to prove useful in later life, when I started to write books.

At Whiteley's, the students spent ten minutes every day on what was called, 'Tots'. This entailed adding up large columns of figures before the bell rang. I was always hopeless at this occupation so it was a big, fat zero for me, every time.

One morning, while at Whiteley's, I received a telephone call from Constance Grant. She wanted to know if I would like to join the chorus of the pantomime at the Lyceum Theatre. Being a Libran, I hate making sudden decisions, so I dithered and said, "I don't know." Miss Grant replied, "That's no good, Pat, I must have a 'yes' or 'no' by tomorrow morning," and rang off. Well, I did decide to join the company of Emile Littler's 'Aladdin' and loved every minute of it.

Sonnie Hale played 'Widow Twanky', Albert Whelan was 'Abanazer' and Eve Lister took the title role. The costumes were really beautiful and I received my first salary from a professional theatrical company - and a first-class one, at that!

Most pantomimes have what is called, a 'Transformation' scene, and in that pantomime it took place in Aladdin's Cave. Lovely sparkling curtains rose, one by one, to reveal the Cave, then we chorus girls entered in long gold-lame dresses, representing, in groups of eight, 'Fame', 'Wealth', and 'Power'. The appropriate attributes were revealed in the jewels, headdresses, and in the items we carried.

I was one of the 'Wealth' girls who carried bows of glittering jewels. One of these bowls also contained four small, round mirrors, and we vied with one another to carry it. Chiefly, I think, because the mirrors caught the lights, so made the person who was carrying it, rather special. At least that was how we saw it at the time. In the end, we took turns to carry it.

We 'Wealth' girls ascended a staircase (off-stage) then walked onto a high rostrum at the back of the stage. Those headdresses were enormous with great plumes of golden feathers. When not in use, they were kept in special wooden boxes, behind the stage.

In the Cave scene, a speciality act called, 'The Diamondos', performed an adagio act. They looked absolutely marvellous, as apart from the necessary 'G' strings, they were covered from head to toe in glittering silver grains. This effect was achieved by smearing a paste onto the skin, then shaking the sparkling specks over it until their entire bodies were covered. They wore rubber caps of the same silvery stuff, and the end result was gorgeous. The spotlights changed colours during their act so that they were bathed in shades of blue, pink, gold, green and purple - it was breathtaking to watch.

As the paste obviously blocked the pores of the skin, it had to be removed after each performance, then re-applied for the next show. In the Finale, they appeared in satin costumes holding glittering masks, so the audience would recognise them.

Whether ''The Diamondos' were a married couple or merely partners, I don't know, but there were always terrible rows going on in their dressing-room. They shouted at each other continuously, which was really rather sad considering the beauty and skill of their act. Perhaps they were fed up with all the hassle and preparation their work entailed. It might even have been the paste on their bodies which affected them in some way.

During the war years there was an absence of tights, so each day we chorus girls applied wet-white to our legs. The Principal Boy also used it. Ours was made from red and yellow ochre, glycerin and water, which was shaken up in a bottle. In spite of the name, 'wet-white', it made our limbs a lovely golden shade and looked good from the front of house.

I was ragged unmercifully because I sometimes went to the theatre wearing one of the gold medals I had won for dancing. The girls told me quite plainly that medals of any kind were of no use in the theatre and no-one took any notice of them. I refrained from pointing out that they had!

Apparently, the only thing that producers and agents were interested in was how an artiste performed on the green (stage). You could have won the greatest award going, but this was of no importance in the theatre. You may be the tops in technical ability, but no earthly use as a *performer*, in projecting yourself to an audience. I was brought very firmly down to earth and left my medals at home. I did inform the girls, however, that training was a necessity for the theatre, whether one entered for competitions, or not.

My parents bought me a smart, leather make-up box, but this object was viewed with much derision. Professionals used a tin box - the older the better, so the gift was replaced by a suitably scruffy-looking cigar box.

Due to the air-raids at night, people stayed indoors, close to their shelters, so we gave performances at the Lyceum at 10-30 a.m., and 2 p.m., and always to full houses. We discovered that you could obtain a smashing lunch at the City Hall. A three course meal for one shilling! So in order to make use of the opportunity we braved the daylight in our stage make-up, which made us look like red Indians. We had no intention of taking it off and re-applying it before the next show, there just wasn't enough time. Everyone stared at us, but as we walked across to the City Hall in groups, we didn't care.

I was asked to understudy the role of the 'Fairy' in the pantomime. I learned her lines and imagined flitting across the stage in a froth of white tulle, but she remained in robust health throughout the run.

Eve Lister, the Principal Boy, wore her black hair in a pageboy style, with a smooth roll across her forehead, and one day all the chorus girls copied her style for a bit of fun. When we came off-stage, the producer, Ernest Duval, with a little twinkle in his eye, said, "Alright girls. Let's put it back the way it was, shall we?" and we screamed with laughter as we clattered up the stairs to our dressing-rooms.

In the finale walk-down, or 'who's best', as it is called in the theatre, everyone came down the steps and acknowledged the applause. But as there were two balconies in the final scene, myself and another girl were instructed to stand on them, one at each side of the stage.

When I saw the other girls walking down I wanted to do the same. I really worried about the problem (for such it was to me), and I tried to think of a way out of it. I decided to speak to the producer, after all he had chosen me as an understudy so he *had* noticed me.

One morning, crossing the darkened stage, I saw Mr. Duval standing in the prompt corner, reading a letter. My legs turned to jelly but I thought, "Here goes, he can only say 'no'". I approached Mr. Duval and asked if I could have a word, and when I received a nod, I told him how much I would like to take a call in the finale with the other girls, and explained the situation. He thought for a moment, then said that in order to avoid pushing past people already on stage, we would have to be first- down the steps, take the call, then exit and proceed to our balconies. That way, as we were wearing large hooped skirts, there would be no collisions. He smiled "Is that better?" I nodded and thanked him, he really was a sweetie.

I told my 'partner' about the new instructions but thought it best to keep the reasons for them to myself, as the girls would no doubt have teased me, again. The head-girl, Brenda, would know about the change, but she never said anything about it.

It was great walking down the steps and taking the applause, and everything went smoothly. That was another lesson I learned. If anything worries you in a show, always speak to your superiors. Even if nothing can be done, at least you will know more about the situation, and the reason for it

18. In my annual pantomime role as Principal Boy.

Although I am unable to recall the lyrics of many shows in which I appeared, I have always remembered those from the opening chorus of my first pantomime at the Lyceum in 1942. They went like this:-

"Hi ya yi yi come and buy, fresh fruit cool and mellow, Hi ya yi yi come and buy, all our wares are cheap today. Rugs and carpets from the East, silks and satins every hue; Fitted for a royal feast, yet available to you. Hi ya yi yi come and buy, fresh fruit cool and mellow. Hi ya yi yi come and buy, all our wares are cheap today. By special edict of the Emperor, whose gracious goodness never, never varies.

Here we meet and chatter, chatter chatter, over the purchase of daily necessaries. Priceless goods and choicest little bits are haggled for by half the population.

In the buzz and babble that befits, the busiest corner of a busy nation. Who will buy, who'll buy, who'll buy, who'll buy?"

The following year, I again joined the pantomime at the Lyceum. This time it was "Babes in the Wood", and I was one of Robin Hood's Merry Men. The Principal Boy was ravishing - tall and blonde with lovely long legs. She noticed the chorus girls, too, and would have a word here and there, and smile at us. Her name was Joy Hayden and she was a well-known actress at the time, although I never heard of her again, after the show finished. During one of the performances, she had a telegram to say her mother had died, and we all felt for her, as she went on stage as if nothing had happened.

I was collecting autographs, and Miss Hayden invited me into her dressing-room. It was all pink and gold with velvet chairs and lots of lights. She gave me a signed photograph, and from that moment I made up my mind that I, too, would become a Principal Boy.

The manager of the chorus asked me if I would like to tour with the Tiller Girls, on a regular basis. One of their scouts had requested her to, "book that vivacious, blonde girl - the one with the long legs." I very much appreciated this interest in me and conveyed my thanks, but rightly or wrongly I relinquished the offer in order to pursue a career as a solo artiste.

Some of the chorus girls were part of Kirby's Flying Ballet and performed wonderful acrobatic feats while floating on wires across the stage. Two of them, Brenda (she was with us, again) and Mabel, actually 'flew' from the stage into the auditorium, somersaulting between the two wires attached to their harnesses, over the astonished patrons in the stalls. I thought they were absolutely brilliant. Twelve years later, when I played Principal Boy at the Empire Theatre, Portsmouth, this unique attraction featured in the production as 'Eugene's Flying Ballet', directed by Arthur Kirby.

The next pantomime at the Lyceum was to be "Cinderella," and I heard that they required one more girl to make up the twenty-four dancers. There were hundreds of pantomimes in those days, in all the major cities and towns; they moved into different theatres every year. Brenda, too, had been sent elsewhere. However, I trotted along to the Stage Door and asked to see the person in charge of the chorus girls, but it was to be another 'third time unlucky' for me. I was told that they had sent to London for a girl and wished I had contacted them, sooner. I wished I had, too! I walked sadly away, the tears streaming down my face, as I thought of all the beautiful costumes and wigs that were worn in "Cinderella", surely the most lavish of pantomimes. Certain that I would never get over this terrible disappointment, I was miserable for many weeks.

Our neighbours in City Road were theatrical people in semi-retirement. Mr. & Mrs. Matthew Glenville had had their own repertory companies, and now, Mr. Glenville was manager of a cinema in Sheffield. His brother Shaun Glenville, a famous pantomime Dame, was the husband of Dorothy Ward. This lady was regarded as the greatest of Principal Boys, and Mrs Glenville would regale me with stories about her sister-in-law and her exciting life. She also made delicious dandelion coffee and taught me how to crochet. I loved the evenings I spent with her.

Mrs. Glenville told me that when Dorothy Ward was invited to a party she always arrived a little late, so that when she eventually put in an appearance, it created a much greater effect. That's show business! I was informed that Dorothy's son, Peter Glenville, was a film director in America. I would sit drinking in the information and the coffee and thinking how wonderful it must be when one is a star.

Mr. Glenville often had to walk home from the cinema during air-raids and was forced to shelter in doorways to avoid shrapnel and falling masonry. When the sirens sounded, my mother would take me and our black spaniel, Judy, to the Glenville's reinforced cellar.

My father was an air-raid warden and would patrol the neighbourhood with other wardens, calling out, "Planes about! Planes about!" One night he popped in to see us and was passing through the Glenville's lounge, when a bomb exploded nearby. The blast blew the radio off it's table and straight into my father's arms. Later, he joined the Local Defence Volunteers, who were known, unkindly, as the "Look, Duck, and Vanish Brigade!"

At last, an Anderson Shelter was installed in our garden. Sunk below ground level, it was covered with the displaced earth and capped with stones. Bunk beds were also provided, so we often spent entire nights in it as it was so much easier than being awakened from sleep by the sirens, and having to make a dash, outside. Several land-mines fell in the vicinity and one destroyed an entire row of new houses. There was just a huge mountain of bricks where they had stood. Windows were covered in criss-cross patterns of black sticky-tape, but most of the windows in the area were shattered, not by bombs, but by a large gun in Manor Lane, called 'Big Bertha'. It caused more damage to the houses than to the enemy aircraft.

Sheffield took a terrible pounding and most of the city centre was flattened. The Moor, a long thoroughfare of buildings and shops was completely destroyed, along with a hotel, for which, in the year previous to the Blitz, my parents had been offered the tenancy. Happily, they had declined.

Marples Hotel, in the centre of the city, was hit by an incendiary bomb and all the customers, including the members of a small orchestra, and the lady violinist, who was a friend of ours, were burned to death. And before the hotel was rebuilt, flowers were regularly placed on the site at each anniversary of the Blitz.

Eight of the Corinthian columns (faced with Darley Dale stone) at the City Hall's impressive entrance, were peppered with shrapnel and splinters. To this day, they remain a lasting reminder of the bombing.

There were stories going round of how people, trapped in cellars, escaped into underground passages that run beneath the city. In earlier times, they provided a means of getting from A to B safely at night, when foot-pads, and other undesirables were abroad.

Recently, one of these passages was discovered, running from Sheffield Castle to the Manor House, the one-time residence of the Earl of Shrewsbury. It must be a very long passage indeed, around a mile in length.

The Turret House, in the grounds of the Manor House, is still extant and is where Mary, Queen of Scots, was held prisoner for seven years. Previously, she had been incarcerated within the cold, stone walls of Sheffield Castle, these being two of the many places she inhabited prior to her execution at Fotheringay.

An historical monument, the Turret House is but a short walk from my home in City Road. This area of Sheffield was once a Deer Park and up to a few years ago, the cellars beneath my house would fill with clear water to a depth of three feet. It was certainly spring water and would disappear as quickly as it had arrived in the space of a few days. Using divining rods, I located the exact spot of this underground spring, as the rods crossed at the same place whether I was in the cellars or the rooms above.

I used to visit the old lady who looked after the Turret House, in which she also lived, as had her parents, previously. She had seven small, black dogs, at one time, and slept on a sofa in front of the kitchen fire, as the building was cold, even in summer.

When visitors called, she would tell them about Mary, and lead them up the winding stone staircase to the Queen's bedroom. This was reached via the prisoner's ladies-inwaiting chamber. 'The Earl of Shrewsbury's coat-of-arms still remains over the fireplace, but the glass case which contained a pair of Mary's gloves and other items belonging to her, disappeared when soldiers were billeted there during the last war. More stairs lead to the flat, leaded roof, where, it is said, soldiers of a bygone age, guarded the Queen when she took the air.

Sometimes, her cousin, Queen Elizabeth 1, allowed Mary to travel to Chatsworth House, and occasionally visit Buton, to take the waters, when she became crippled with rheumatism.

However, she was always carefully guarded.

I took Judy my spaniel for regular walks and one day I chose a route which skirted Norfolk Park; the entrance to a farm, then crossed a field, via stiles, to a clearing edged with Elder trees. While playing with my dog, I noticed a man lurking behind a bush and something warned me to depart at once, ignoring the stranger, I regained the path and proceeded through the field until I neared the farm entrance. The man, however, had a bicycle and by riding along a path, gained the entrance to the farm before I did. I thought it better to walk rather than run, so nonchalantly throwing sticks for Judy, I climbed over the final stile. Out of the corner of my eye, I saw the man standing in the shadow of a tree, exposing himself. I knew that I was in great danger, but I continued walking steadily until I reached the road where the houses started.

Once safely back at home, and as my parents were out, I locked the doors and fastened all the windows. While I was upstairs, I heard the sound of approaching footsteps, then someone knocking on the front door! I did not move. I could not.

Alter a while the knocking stopped, and I heard voices. Mrs. Grenville was calling me, over the wall, so I opened my bedroom window to hear what she was saying. "Oh, there you lire, Pat. Are you alright? A gentleman has followed you from the park." "I know," I said, "but he won't get into this house!" My friend exclaimed, "No, no. He wants to know if you are alright because he has been watching a man who was following you. He hid behind a tree in the park and saw what the man was doing." The penny dropped. So, another man had been spying on the man with the bike! "Oh dear. Thank him for me, will you?" I said. "Tell him I'm fine, now." Nevertheless I stayed safely indoors and never met my good Samaritan.

There was a real to-do when my parents came home, and they said I was not to go anywhere near the fields, again, unless I was accompanied by someone. I think I had a lucky escape that day.

During the war years, I played a few of the smaller clubs, and several male artistes thought it would be a good idea for me to team up with then in a double act. These offers were declined, kindly, but firmly. However there was one musician with whom

I worked, briefly, and I think this came about because I had worked with his daughter at the Lyceum.

Bert Carlton was a classical violinist who also played a curious instrument called a musical saw. He achieved this by placing the handle of the saw between his knees and bending it into various positions while drawing the violin bow across the blade. He accompanied me when I sang but I was rather embarrassed at being seen on stage with a man so much older than myself, and the act was disbanded.

I wanted to work the entire Sheffield club circuit, but this was a whole new ball-game. To enter this mysterious world, you had to attend the Trades Hall club every Thursday evening, in order to obtain engagements.

Many theatrical artistes worked the clubs in-between theatre dates and some of them even took up permanent residence in Sheffield. If you had a good act, you were assured of continuous engagements for many years. In those days, however, it was considered to be slightly *infra dig.* to work the clubs at all, and theatrical managements were against the idea, so artistes used a different name in clubland.

My mother and I had our own little spot in the Trades Hall and because my club name was 'Pat Crosby', it came to be known as 'Crosby Corner'. Concert secretaries for miles around would ring the Trades Hall for acts, and a list of names would be read out to them. The act (or acts) they chose, was then called out to go to the 'phone. Soon, my name began to be called out, frequently, and some of the artistes would groan when I appeared, as they thought there would be less chances for them. But actually, lots of bookings were arranged on those nights, and most people went home, satisfied.

I would cringe every time we entered the Trades Hall. Again, it was *entering* a room full of people that I hated, but once safety inside, I was completely at ease. Often, having been booked for several clubs quite quickly, my mother and I did not have to stay very long. This was before the days of the agents who became the middle-men.

Slim Farrell, a portly gent, was the first agent to book artistes for clubs in the Sheffield area, but he was barred from engaging in this occupation at the Trades Hall. We artistes were against paying an agent when we could obtain work over the club's telephone. So, Slim would sit in the window of the café next door, and beckon to acts as they passed by. Some of them were seduced in this way, but most artistes ignored the beckoning hand - myself included.

I was offered two weeks in Hull with another act, Johnnie Pedlar (comedian/impressionist), and as Johnnie was known lo my parents as a 'respectable family-man', I was allowed to go there, unchaperoned. But Johnnie became quite ill while wo were in Hull, and I worked some of the dates on my own. He lay in his bedroom looking positively green, so I laid cool cloths on his fevered brow and gave him iced water to drink.

Recently, a man approached me while I was out shopping, and said, "Do you remember me? I'm Johnnie Pedlar. We worked together in Hull, a long time ago." It took a minute or two, then I smiled, and nodded. He went on, "When you are on television, I tell my family that you looked after me when I was ill and made a good little nurse, but they don't believe me!" I have known so many people from different walks of life, that I don't always recognise them unless, like Johnnie, they speak to me. They always seem to know me. It must be a case of once seen, never forgotten!

The clubs in Hull had excellent bands with at least six musicians in them. This was a rare treat for club artistes, as those elsewhere were usually confined to a pianist, and (if you were lucky), a drummer.

The musicians in Hull easily accompanied the classical pieces I played such as the "Tritsch-tratsch Polka" and the "Sabre Dance". Popular numbers were reserved for my final act of the evening, and my vocals included "Hear my Song, Violetta", and "Santa Lucia". Both our acts went over well and for me, it was the first of many subsequent visits.

I played the plush Excelsior Club at Grimsby, several times, and took a shine to the trombone-player in the band. On one of my return bookings, I invited my mother to stay the week with me at the nearby resort of Cleethorpes, and during the week, Tony, my musician friend, asked me to attend a dance with him at the Pier Pavilion Ballroom. Mother stipulated that I be brought straight back after the dance, and off we went. I thoroughly enjoyed that week as it had the added stimulation of a little flirtation into the bargain.

Some time later, when I was away from home, my parents told me that a large crate of fresh fish had arrived from my admirer in Grimsby! It was very hot weather just then, and as it was before the days of domestic refrigerators, my parents gave most of it away to friends. When my Aunt Annie called, she was presented with the last of the fish and took it away with her. I gathered that it had become a little 'high' by then, as my aunt later complained that she was followed home on the tram-car by a large number of blowflies!

Sheffield clubs came in all shapes and sizes. Woodhouse Mill was unusual, in that there were two rooms in operation – one upstairs, so acts performed two spots in each room. If you were the only act on the bill, most clubs required four appearances a night, but the larger ones had as many as three artistes, where two spots would suffice.

Some acts were paid up after their first appearances. This meant that the members did not like them, so they were given their fee and asked to leave. Several artistes who came up from London, returned there very quickly indeed!

Sheffield-born comedienne and suerstar, Marti Caine, who so sadly died at the age of 50, started her career in the clubs. At one venue in Leeds, a man in the audience continually heckled her, but sharp as a razor Marti looked down at him and said, "Do you mind! I like to do my act the same way you have your sex - ALONE!"

One of my favourite dates was the Limes Club, on Barnsley Road. The concert secretary was Horace Whetton, who with his wife, Irene Mellor also had a professional singing act.

They were both trained singers. Irene was tiny, with flaming-red hair. She often wore a dramatic gown composed of yards of white satin, with a huge corsage of violets. Horace, in full evening-dress, made an admirable foil for her.

Their daughter, Mary Millar, followed in her parents' foot-steps with a theatrical career. In recent years, I was delighted to see her on television, as 'Rose', in "Keeping up Appearances", a hilarious, situation comedy. It is so good to see this kind of success, especially for Mary, whose parents were friends of mine.

The Chairman at Woodhouse Central Club was quite a card. He would announce me over the microphone: "Now, come on, give order, you've got a grand turn tonight." Then, when the noise had subsided, turn in my direction, and add, "Come on, Pat, duck." The term 'duck' being an endearment, which to my mind completely ruined his attempt at a 'build-up'.

A lady once came up to me in the street, and remarked, "I remember you on the clubs. My husband and I used to come and see you, wherever you appeared." So, I had two fans - at least!

An excellent comedienne was paid up in some outlandish place and asked the Concert Secretary if there was a back way out. "No," he replied, "you mun go through't front and tak yer chance!"

Some club members, such as those at the Sheffield Foundry Workers, could not applaud an act, even if they wished to do so, as their hands were rough and sore from the work they did. Being unaware of this, I thought I had 'died the death' when they clanked their glasses on the tables. Then someone told me that this was *their* way of showing appreciation. So having stayed in the dressing-room feeling awful, I was able to emerge with some relief.

One club had a microphone which began slowly and agonisingly to slide down while I was singing. As I was accompanying myself on the accordion at the time, there was nothing I could do about it.

In most clubs, it was difficult to be heard without amplification, even if you had a strong voice, as the acoustics were the last thing in mind when they were built. It was often said that you took your life in your hands when you played the clubs; and of notorious ones, that if they liked you they let you live!

The late and great comedian, Sandy Powell, who played the theatres all his life, developed two speciality acts in which he satirised a magician and a ventriloquist. They were hilarious! Sandy presented both sketches on television and gave one or two special shows in the Sheffield area. The audience at one club, however, missed the point and thought his acts, in which everything went wrong, were for real. When Sandy went to the bar for a drink, he overheard a man say, "I thought 'e was a bad conjurer, but 'e's a bloody sight worse as a vent!" A case of throwing pearls before swine?

Sandy used to say, "They're going to close the Empire Theatre, Swansea, and if its a success, they're going to close all the others." He was born in Rotherham, and after his death, a new hotel in that town was named, "The Comedian", in Sandy Powell's honour.

I played Southey Social Club, and the concert-room was daunting. It was another aircraft hanger! The week prior to the engagement, we perused the local magazine, "Our Clubs", and discovered I was on the bill with a female vocal duo, and Ronnie Dukes. Now, Ronnie was very popular as an entertainer, and people followed him round wherever he appeared -a sort of mobile fan-club.

A few days before the date, my mother came in with a new copy of music - "The Harry Lime Theme", from the film, "The Third Man", all the rage at the time. A catchy, and surprisingly easy piece to play, I soon memorised it, and by employing certain musical effects, got the most out of the music, as it were. I decided to try it out at Southey, in the lunch-time show. These 'noon' shows had all-male audiences as a rule; the women staying at home and preparing the Sunday dinner.

The duo went on first, and received a smattering of polite applause. They were new to the business, and I'm afraid, did sing a little out of tune - at least, one of them did. I followed them, and gave my dots (music), to the band. I opened with

"Amparita Roca", a stirring, Spanish march; sang "Hear my song, Violetta", then announced the "Harry Lime Theme". The band gave me good backing, and at the end, the entire concert-room erupted. They loved it! At the evening show, it went over 'a bomb', and I had to play it again as an encore. Ronnie, of course, went well, but I had the edge that day, and I gave my mother a special hug for buying me that sheet of music.

I was bathed in a lovely warm glow. It is so wonderful when your work is well received. As I packed up my dresses, I thought of my terror that first night at Dial House Social Club, and how much things had changed, and I said to myself - "So far, so good!"

Chapter 2
The Smell of the Greasepaint

I was introduced to a comedian by the name of Ernie Payne, who put on variety bills in the theatres and produced summer shows and pantomimes. He booked me for two engagements, the first being a week in Variety at the Theatre Royal, Loughborough - my debut as a solo artiste in a proper theatre.

My mother took me to Loughborough and saw me fixed up in a clean boarding-house, then she went home. I was alone and going to be - 'on the stage'! I suffered very much from homesickness, which is something like *mal de mare* without actually throwing-up. It is, however, equally horrible.

Single acts that worked in Variety had a lonely life on the whole, as unlike Revue, where the same artistes were together for months or even years, Variety bills were mostly composed of different acts every week. I much preferred Revue for that, and other reasons.

Again, in Revue, a Musical Director travelled with the show, and took charge of the Band Call on Monday mornings, but in Variety, you took the orchestra through your music, personally, and if you were late, you had to join the queue, as all the band parts were laid out on the stage. It was a case of first come, first served. You also had to be familiar with the lighting plot for your act and were required to inform the electricians as to the colours you required.

For an important number, usually near the end of your act, the stage would be darkened, with only a strong, white spotlight upon you. When your act finished, the instructions read, 'F.U.F', which meant 'Full up finish', when every available light would be switched on - the cue for applause. These mysteries, however, were unknown to me. Then.

For my act at Loughborough, I wore a medieval-type red velvet dress and a cloak of self-doubt. I sang "The Pipes of Pan" at the piano, and a ballad, "Love, here is my heart", with the orchestra, and I certainly did not tear up any trees.

One night, the grand piano started to move slowly towards the footlights. There was a sharp rake on that stage, and the blocks, used to stabilise the instrument, had been forgotten. I moved my stool in order to keep up with the piano's progress and felt sick. It stopped a few inches from the apron of the stage, and the orchestra, with visions of being crushed beneath the heavy Bechstein, was saved from having music on the brain!

My salary was £7 a week, so with two pounds ten shillings for board and lodgings, I could spend a little, and save the remainder.

I was booked by the same management for my first summer season at Saltburn-by-the-Sea in North Yorkshire. This proved to be a very difficult time for me, due to the mother of one Marie Joy, another act in the show. Mrs. Morgan was a Welsh dragon of the most fearsome kind. She made all Marie's costumes and hated any other act which she considered might take the limelight away from her daughter. Marie, was a pretty, petite soubrette, ruled with a rod of iron.

Being new to the business, my mother had asked Mrs. Morgan to keep an eye on me, so I stayed in the same lodgings as Mrs. M. and Marie.

Saltburn has lovely street names, such as 'Emerald', 'Pearl' and 'Diamond', and we stayed in Ruby Street. The landlady offered terribly from B.O., and whenever her huge bulk hove into view, I quickly grabbed my handkerchief.

Because I was the only other young, blonde artiste, I was soon on the receiving end of Mrs. M's devious mind, and a hate campaign ensued. I became very unhappy and longed to leave the show. When I was singing, heavy items were dropped backstage and I was fast becoming a nervous wreck.

My mother came over, and I was so relieved to see her. She obtained employment as manageress of the nearby Tea-Gardens Cafe, and life became easier. I had tried to explain my situation to Ernie Payne, but he was just not interested and said I was imagining it all.

There was a sequel to Marie and Mrs. M., but first I must mention Marie's boyfriend. Mrs. M. was always talking of this young man. His stage-name was 'Rondart', and he was going to marry her daughter. He was tall and good-looking, and had a marvellous speciality act in which he blew darts from his mouth, onto a dartboard. As a silent act, he worked all over the world.'Rondart' came to Saltburn for a Sunday concert, with another artiste, Tuppy Oliver, the sister of the Australian star, Vic Oliver.

However, several years later, I was touring in a revue, and we played a theatre in Birmingham. The comedian, Dick Montague, and his wife, Penny, complained of feeling tired all the time. I sympathised, and enquired if they knew the cause, and Dick said, "Well, its where we are standing this week." (They owned a luxury, touring caravan.) It appeared that the people in a caravan close to their own, argued and fought all night so sleep was impossible. It was Mrs. M. and Marie! Apparently, Marie was now married (but not to 'Rondart') and they all lived together in a caravan. Dick said that the vehicle shook and swayed, alarmingly, during their fights. The Welsh dragon was still breathing fire!

I have had a number of falls in my life, and a spectacular one occurred after the final performance of a pantomime in Manchester. My mother had come over to help me pack up, etc; and I suddenly remembered my photographs in the foyer of the theatre. I ran through the darkened auditorium, turned a corner, and plunged down into nothingness. It was a series of stairs which led to an exit! I screamed once, then hit the concrete at the bottom.

They came to look for me holding lighted matches, as the front-of-house lighting had been turned off at the mains. I was lucky, in that I was still alive and only sustained a badly broken wrist. A broad, silver bracelet I was wearing at the time, was severely dented, but may have protected my wrist from worse damage.

I lost consciousness for a while and was eventually taken to a hospital where they bandaged the wrist and advised me to attend a hospital in Sheffield, as soon as possible. That night, rather than 'bringing the house down', the 'house' brought *me* down!

At the Royal Hospital in Sheffield, they put a pot on my arm, just as it was, all funny and twisted and agonisingly painful. And because the pain failed to abate, I went back to the hospital. A Sister sniffed, "You should not be here. It's too early to take off the pot." But my mother insisted upon seeing the specialist and said we would wait. The Sister, shrugged, and stalked off.

When it was our turn to go in, the Orthopaedic Consultant looked at the original X-Ray then said I had better have the I plaster off and go up to the operating-theatre, as the bones must be set, again. I refrained from informing him that my wrist had not been set the first time! I had this awful mask put over my face, and before I went under, my breathing sounded like a hurricane in my ears, as I fought for air.

When I came round, there was a new, slimmer-style plaster on my arm and the pain was excruciating. But thanks are due to my mother for insisting upon seeing the consultant that day. If the bones has not been properly set there is no doubt I would have lost the use of my hand, and among other things, my ability to play the accordion. However, after much physiotherapy, it was as good as new. Recently, I broke the other wrist, so I now have a matching pair!

While my arm was in plaster, I fulfilled my engagements in Sheffield minus the accordion, and when I arrived at Walkley Workingmen's Club, I discovered that Marie Joy was on the same bill! Nevertheless, it was an entirely different kettle of fish from the Saltburn scenario, as I now had more confidence in myself, and also more experience.

Mrs. M. was installed in the small dressing-room for the entire evening, and as far as I can recall, nothing much was said apart from the usual courtesies of 'Hello' and 'Goodbye', with accent on the latter.

The club members knew that I also played the accordion, as I was frequently booked there, but I must say that my singing went down as well, if not better, than on previous occasions. Perhaps they felt sorry for me, with my arm in plaster and all. Marie was also well received, but it was *my act* which gained cries of 'Encore!'

When I came off stage, Mrs. M.'s glances were daggers, and of course I preened a bit, enjoying my victory to the full. I 'put it on' and rubbed salt into the wound! After all, she had made my life a misery at Saltburn, and now, as far as I was concerned, the scales were balanced. I never met them again.

A minor 'falling' incident occurred during a pantomime at the Lyceum Theatre in Sheffield, when I was one of Robin Hood's Merry Men. As we marched bravely onto the stage, the girl in front of me, caught her foot in the floor covering. She managed to keep her balance, but I fell over the piece that was now sticking up, and dropped my bow, too. I was back on my feet in a trice, so the hiatus was not too noticeable.

Twelve years later, when I played the part of 'Robin Hood' myself, at the Empire Theatre, in Portsmouth, I hit the deck, once again. It was the final performance, and the theatre was full, with standing-room only, available. On these last night's of shows, things can go haywire, as the comedians tend to play tricks on each other. They finished some gag or other and made their exit. Then I strode on and fell sideways with a resounding crash. The comedians had been messing about with a bucket of water, and some of it had spilled onto the stage. The heel of my boot found it and slipped from under me.

When something like this happens in a theatre, there are usually only two reactions from an audience. One is hysterical laughter, and the other, a shocked and concerted sound of 'Ooooh!', long drawn out. Happily, I was the recipient of the latter, as I jumped up and continued with my lines. Despite my bruised and aching body, I stood in the finale line-up, smiling, and clutching bouquets and baskets of fruit, feeling a million dollars.

Once, while working in cabaret, the heel of my shoe came off and I crashed onto the ballroom floor. It was nearly always a 'full body slam' every time.

A second summer season found me at Exmouth in the lovely county of Devon; this time for a London management. Wally Watson (the comedian in the show), Ninon (a French vocalist), and myself, stayed in a large Victorian house in Rolles Road. It was beautifully furnished and had two other paying guests. One of these was a rather mannish, elderly lady, complete with pince-nez, cropped hair, shirt and tie. When meeting her in one of the corridors, she would utter a sharp, "Oh!", as though surprised to see me, then pass by without a word. The other person was a sweet little grey-haired lady called Mary Heaton. She would invite me into her large, sunny room, which was filled with roses. Their perfume was intoxicating. Her greeting was usually, "A-ha", uttered in a girlish treble.

Returning to the house after the show, Wally would walk up the drive, then move quickly sideways, disappearing behind a bush. He would then pop out with an "Oh!", or a "A-ha", as the fancy took him, while Ninon and I fell about.

A major fault with this establishment was that of cockroaches which infested the bathrooms and sometimes even the bedrooms! Ninon was forever setting out on forages, armed with a weapon in the shape of one of her high-heeled shoes. I was terrified of them and screamed the house down when I discovered one in the sheets of my bed.

Wally always called me, 'Patricia Grimesthorpe Dawson' because he had this thing about a theatre he once played at Grimesthorpe, a particularly drab district of Sheffield, back in 1900 and frozen to death. It made no difference when I explained that I lived nowhere near the wretched place.

Ninon often called me, 'Patricia - what's the time, girls? - Dawson' Apparently, I posed this question in the dressing-room, more than was deemed necessary! One day, someone rushed in to say that Pat Kirkwood was in the audience and sitting on the front row! Pat Kirkwood was a famous actress and there she sat with her mother and aunt, looking very lovely in a sunny, yellow dress, the perfect foil for her long dark hair and sun-tan. She smiled and clapped every act, enthusiastically.

After a pantomime in which I played, 'Fairy', I was booked as a speciality act in Frank H. Fortescue's production of "Goldilocks and the Three Bears". Fortescue had repertory companies throughout the North of England, and although his pantomimes included people from the legitimate theatre, variety acts would also be engaged.

The producer, the eminent T. Mostoll Willey, was a dear man, and his daughter, Joan Francis, played the title role. We opened at Her Majesty's Theatre, Carlisle, and the cast was very friendly and pleasant to work with and made me feel 'at home'. The girl who played the 'Fairy', fell in love with the 'Demon King'. On stage, they were antagonists - good, fighting evil, but elsewhere they were always in each other's arms. Joan Francis was later to star as 'Dot Greenhalgh' in "Coronation Street", that long-running television soap and addiction of the British people. I, too, appeared in it, disguised as various characters - once, as a prostitute.

Joan would regale Patricia Phoenix (Elsie Tanner in 'the Street'), with stories of how I 'wowed' them in pantomime and stopped the show. Her flattering comments apart, I thought the world of Joan, she was a lovely person. But, as so often happens in the theatre world, friends become separated, although I did meet up with her again, a few years later.

At, Granada's Television Studios in Manchester, Pat Phoenix always admired my jewellery. She even offered me £50 for carnelian, entaglio ring, set in gold, but I was not tempted.

On the set of 'the Street', I renewed my friendship with Arthur Leslie who played 'Jack Walker'. Arthur and I were twice in the same pantomime, where he took the part of 'Baron Hardup'. Sadly, both Pat and Arthur have now passed away.

Eventually, I received a contract to play Principal Boy for Fortescue, and T. Mostoll Willey (Tommy), had a hand in this. I mentioned my ambition to play 'Boy' to Tommy and asked what he thought of my chances. He said that he could not see any serious obstacles and would broach the subject to Frank when next they met. Then, seeing my doubtful expression, added, "I have said I will talk to him, and I will, never fear."

The pantomime ended its run, and I forgot about the conversation until one day I received a telephone call from Edith Carter, Fortescue's personal secretary. She enquired if I would be free to play 'Boy' in "Goldilocks" for the coming season. Would

I just! A contract was duly signed, and I stayed with that management for a further five years. I had fulfilled a major ambition.

The first time I strode onto the stage as 'Prince Valentine of Sundown', was at the Hippodrome Theatre, in Wigan. It was a beautiful theatre, and the cast was appreciative of the spacious facilities and the well-equipped dressing-rooms. The 'newish' feel of the Hippodrome seemed in harmony with my new role, and during my speciality act, another unfamiliar thing occurred. When I started playing, "12th Street Rag", the entire brass section of the orchestra stood up, and really 'went to town' with the number. The audience thundered their approval- clapping and cheering, as I doffed my cap - a winning ploy thought up on the spur of the moment.

The musicians spontaneous actions were gloriously uplifting, although it was to be the only time I ever encountered this type of enthusiasm. Nevertheless, it was all grist to the mill, and I continued my love affair with the audience.

When speaking lines, the voice had to carry to the back of the auditorium, as amplification was then unknown. And in most productions it was necessary to have a good singing voice, and the ability to dance reasonably well. I soon realised the importance of my early training, and appreciated my parents all the more for giving me the opportunity to develop these talents. Not to mention the financial cost, involved in it all.

The following week we played the Palace Theatre in Attercliffe, Sheffield, and although it was not half so grand as the Lyceum or the Empire, it was always well patronised, providing a show gained the approval of those who attended at the beginning of the week. Word was soon passed round of a production's worth and would be the guiding factor for box-office takings.

Many artistes who played the Palace went on to become big names. My father's impression of a young comedian who specialised in eccentric dancing, was that he would go to the top. His opinion was justified when Billy Dainty became a star.

Naturally, I lived at home during that week, but I became very ill and developed tonsillitis, with a temperature of 103 degrees! The faithful Doctor Billington was called in, and after examining me, shook his head: "Dear, dear, what are we to do with you. You are not fit to get out of this bed, and as for performing on stage ..." I explained as best I could, that there were no understudies in the pantomime, and I could not let them down. He sighed and painted my throat with some obnoxious substance in order to shrink the swollen tonsils. It was agony.

After each night's delirious sleep, I awoke to the realisation of my awful predicament; peer at my bright red face in the mirror, and groan. The fever made me light-headed and unsteady on my feet, and my parents were sick with worry. I could not believe such bad luck after that wonderful time in Wigan. Was it only a week ago?

Every day I stayed in bed until the last possible moment, then heaved myself up to await the taxi and repeat the terrible battle. I don't know how I was able to sing a single note, but some sort of sounds came out. Who invented that stupid saying; 'the show must go on'?

I played the Palace again in happier times and will always remember the orchestra. At the end of every performance, they would stand up, face the audience, and sing the following song:

> *"Cheerio until the next time*
> *At the Palace, Attercliffe.*
> *May the skies be always blue*
> *And all your wonderful dreams come true.*
> *Health and happiness, we pray,*
> *May forever with you stay - so*
> *Cheerio until the next time*
> *At the Palace, Attercliffe."*

Then the Musical Director, who always wore white, holey, Mickey Mouse gloves, leapt over the handrail and ran to the end of the orchestra pit, where he would play a solo on the tubular bells. Upon his return, to conduct while the people left the theatre, he would ask, "What page are we at?" and the band would reply, "Page twelve, you bloody fool!"

On tour, you remembered a town for a particular idiosyncrasy associated with one of its theatres. For example, the King's Palace, Preston, had lots of white tiles, just like a loo. And at the Empire Theatre, Belfast, the orchestra had a huge net suspended over them, to prevent the debris, hurled onto the stage from 'the Gods' (balcony), from hitting them! At the Queen's Park Hippodrome in Manchester, a man who frequented the theatre bar, always ate the glasses! I was taken through the pass door to witness this phenomenon. He would crunch his way through a large, thick-handled jar, order another pint, drink it, then eat that glass, too! I could not see the sense in this occupation, unless it was *his* way of gaining an audience.

About this time, I had a crush on Jack Isherwood, who played 'Simple Simon' in the pantomime. He was a repertory artiste and married to my friend, Joan Francis. Really, it was all in my mind, but being a Libran, I obtained happiness from my imagination, and that was enough. Of course, I was thrilled when Jack once kissed me 'goodnight' - I was on a high for days. But despite one or two heart-throbs and enthusiasms, I remained a virgin until the age of twenty-five.

The doctor sent me to a specialist to have my beastly tonsils removed. It was arranged quite quickly, and apart from a haemorrhage after returning home, the operation was successful. The bleeding was frightening, however, and after filling a large basin with blood, the steadfast Doctor Billington was called from his bed. As there was no ice available, he said that the only thing to do was to lie very quietly without moving and pray for it to stop. If it continued, I would have to return to hospital for my throat to be stitched. This dire warning may have helped, as the bleeding eventually ceased. Just before my operation, one of the porters at the hospital recognised me and told the surgeon I was a singer. "Then, let us hope she can sing after this," was his caustic reply.

My voice did not return for several months, and an audition loomed for the B.B.C. at Broadcasting House in Leeds, so I wrote to request another appointment. However, they offered me an appointment earlier than the original one, so I decided to risk it.

For the audition, I chose to sing, "On Wings of Song", and "Santa Lucia" followed by an accordion solo, "12th Street Rag". Ken Frith from the B.B.C. Northern Variety Orchestra, accompanied me expertly on the piano, but I was so nervous that I forgot to release the lower button on the bellows of my instrument, and realised this as soon as I started to play. One good thing about the error was that it helped to keep the music under the voice, but I quickly rectified this mistake for the accordion solo.

A letter from the B.B.C. stated that I would be called for a further test in due course, and this occurred during a summer show at Mablethorpe. With difficulty, I managed to keep this second appointment.

At this second audition, Barney Colehan and five nameless beings were closeted in a listening box in the depths of Broadcasting House. When it was over, Barney immediately offered me a contract with "Have a Go", a popular radio show due to record its 5th series that Autumn of 1950.

The programme featured Wilfred Pickles, a famous broadcaster, who started his career in radio as a newscaster. This was a highly unusual event due to the fact that he spoke with a Yorkshire accent. He was aided in "Have a Go", by Barney Colehan (the producer), and Violet Carson, who played the piano. Violet, later went on to become a legend in "Coronation

Street", as the frosty, sharp-tongued,'Ena Sharples'. Barney confided to me that only one artiste in two hundred ever passed an audition at the B.B.C., so I returned to Mablethorpe on top of the world!

A few days after the season ended, I boarded a train for London and my first engagement for 'Auntie' B.B.C. After checking in at my hotel, I was taken in a chauffeur-driven limousine, which glided smoothly through the city's traffic, to Broadcasting House in Piccadilly. There, we picked up Violet Carson, and proceeded to the Port of London Authority, Millwall Docks, where the first recording of "Have a Go" was to take place.

Here in person was Violet Carson, sitting beside me in the car's luxurious upholstery. She was already a well-known artiste, and I had often heard her on the radio. Violet, however, rather spoiled my first impression of her by hastening to inform me that I was not to worry if my act failed to impress the audience, as they only wanted to see Wilfred, anyway. This remark did absolutely nothing for my confidence. As it was, my nerves were beginning to show.

The large canteen was packed with people. Flowers were arranged round the front of the stage, which for sound recording was thickly carpeted. After several trips to the ladies powder-room, it was nearly time to go on. The compere, Pat Woodings, asked if I would follow Violet, with Gerard Peters (a baritone), following me. I stammered agreement and swallowed on a dry throat, as I strapped on my accordion.

Violet sang some Lancashire folk songs at the piano; took her rather polite applause and disappeared. It was then that I recalled her remark in the car, and I was suddenly determined to do well. "Here goes,' I thought, as I heard Pat introduce me in his marvellous, cultured voice, and I sailed on to a sea of faces. "Have a Go" involved audience participation, so there was no dimming of the house lights. My song finished to a roar of approval - even cries of "Encore" and after a selection on the accordion, I received tumultuous applause. It was several minutes before Pat was able to introduce Gerard.

19. Violet Carson, self and Dorothy Bickerdike (Barney Colehan's secretary), on the O'Connell Bridge in Dublin (Oct 1950). Violet said, "look miserable, then he will not take our picture." Wrong!

The B.B.C. in their wisdom, had confined my contract to the first programme, when I was 'on trial' so to speak. But contracts for the entire series quickly followed. I overheard Violet commenting to someone from the B.B.C., "Oh, you won't want me, now that you have someone young and pretty," and thought, "What a load of rhubarb." Still, I suppose it was a kind of back-handed compliment.

The next morning, Barney remarked, "You did extremely well last night. By the way, may we call you, 'Paddy'?" He explained that there could be some confusion with the other 'Pat' (Pat Woodings), so I was 'Paddy' for the rest of the tour. Actually, when I was born, Doctor Callaghan said, "Why not call her 'Paddy'? She looks a real 'Paddy' to me." A play entitled "Paddy - The Next Best Thing!" was running at the time, so my parents were never sure whether his comment was intended as a compliment, or not!

In Wexford, Eire, we stayed at Whites Hotel where the food was fantastic. The programme was recorded in the town's Theatre Royal, which had been dark for some years. After the show, a party was held at the hotel for the local dignitaries and the people who had helped to arrange it. Monks from a nearby abbey were invited too, and stood around in brown girdled robes, their tonsured heads gleaming with perspiration. They drank whiskey and smoked cigars with the best of 'em.

I was cornered by a priest, Father Gaul, who proceeded to adopt a fatherly attitude to me (as one would expect), while plying me with drinks. He was quite sweet, really, and next morning appeared on the station platform clutching a bunch of violets. He pressed them into my hands, and as the train moved away, said he hoped we would meet again, very soon. Alas, his hopes were unfulfilled.

Irish trains were a law unto themselves and mostly moved at n snail's pace This allowed passengers to jump out and collect wild strawberries, growing at the side of the track. Pat Woodings was actually permitted to drive the train for a while, and returned, grimy, but immensely satisfied, having achieved one of his dearest ambitions.

Apart from Wilfred, Mabel and Barney, who travelled in their own compartment, the rest of us always played cards on train journeys. Violet and I became quite good friends as we were both interested in antiques and would search a particular town for worthwhile treasures. Once, in Chester, we came across a shop where a crowd had gathered and were peering through the windows. Curious, we peered in, too, and saw Wilfred and Mabel inside. We grinned at each other as we walked away. This was one of the prices to be paid for fame.

On board ship, returning from Ireland, Wilfred bought me my first Guinness, but it was too bitter for my taste. I much preferred milk stout in those days. Wilfred liked his whiskey; a high colour, and a constant twinkle in his eye, betrayed this predilection.

Wilfred's birthday was the 13th of October, with Barney's secretary's on the 12th, my own on the 14th, and Mabel's on the 16th. What one might call a loquacity of Librans!

At the time of these Solar Returns we were staying at the Penhelig Arms in Aberdovey, where a celebration was deemed necessary. But when most of us had retired for the night, the sounds of an accordion could be heard in the lower regions. Next day, I wanted to know the identity of the midnight musician, and Alun Williams from B.B.C. Cardiff, said that he was the culprit and had played my accordion for a while. Well, I was definitely not amused. In the theatrical profession, it is unheard of even to touch an artiste's instrument, especially without their permission, and I told Alun so in no uncertain terms. He apologised profusely, even suggesting to show me round Aberdovey (an expedition which would have taken all of fifteen minutes!), but my feathers were decidedly ruffled, and after that incident kept the accordion, when not in use, in my bedroom. It was worrying, because if anything had happened to it, an accidentally spilt drink for example, I could not have fulfilled my contract.

While in Aberdovey, we were invited on board a vessel anchored in the harbour and employed in the training course of the Aberdovey Sea School for Boys, for whom "Have a Go!" was being presented that evening. The tide was out and the ship lay low in the water. Descent to the deck was via a rope ladder and involved the feat of swinging yourself round to the other side of the contraption, halfway down. I thought I would have to let go and crash to the deck, where a sea of upturned faces awaited our arrival. I do not know how I managed to hold onto the rope, as my hands, supporting most of my weight, were aching to release their burden. Amazingly, Violet, senior in age to me, and of larger proportions performed the feat quite easily.

In Liverpool, I swanned around the Adelphi Hotel, feeling rather grand. Everybody who was somebody, stayed there. You can easily get lost in that hotel, so we arranged a place and a time to meet up - usually in the cocktail bar. Wilfred and Mabel were always looked after, hand and foot, so I imagine it was similar to being in the retinue of royalty. And when we arrived in Milium, Cumbria, the children in the town were given the day off from school so that they could stand waving Union Jacks as we glided past in our gleaming limousines.

Initially, I was booked as an accordionist. Barney said it would make a nice change to have music between the vocalists, i.e. Violet and Gerard. But I stuck to my guns, determined to sing at least one number, as it was part of my act and I enjoyed it. So, Barney capitulated and said, "Well O.K., but just the one, mind." And that was fine by me.

We played a cinema at Heckmondwike, in Yorkshire, where the audience wanted more, and I thought, "No one can stop me while I am on stage," and went into another song. Later, I received the expected ticking-off from the producer, although he was nice about it. Barney explained that the timing of the show was a big consideration and I must not be so naughty, again. I promised, never again, but it was well worth the reprimand.

The summer of 1951 was spent in Holyhead (Holy Head), on the island of Anglesey. Actually, Holyhead is situated on a tiny island called Holy Island, separated from Anglesey by a road bridge. To join this show I went to London for an interview and asked my mother to accompany me. The interview was successful and a signed contract was tucked inside my handbag, so I suggested that we had a wee dram by way of a celebration.

Popping into the nearest hotel, we relaxed in a lounge, resting tired feet and talking about our day, when the unexpected happened. We were interrupted by a smartly-dressed female who appeared at our table and enquired if we had just arrived in London. Mystified, we nodded, and asked what she wanted. The stranger said that if my mother agreed, she would take care of me and introduce me to some people who would be interested in me. The penny dropped with a loud clang! She was obviously touting for 'talent'. Mother, immediately gave the woman the length of her tongue, and our visitor glided back to her seat without another word. We finished our drinks, leisurely, not wishing to appear bothered by the incident, but I was glad when we left the establishment. Mother commented, "Well, would you believe it! You will have to stay somewhere, suitable when you rehearse for this show, or your father and I will not know a moment's peace."

When the time came, I stayed at the Theatre Girls Club in Greek Street, Soho. It was ideal for girls who were rehearsing in

London, being central, and run on strict disciplinarian lines. Each girl made her own bed, washed her own utensils and had to be indoors before 7p.m. The meals were adequate if a trifle plain and consisted of breakfast and a nice hot supper. The club was a sturdy, stone building with large windows, and you had to ring the bell in order to gain entry, as the large green door was always locked against intruders.

Dancers, singers, and actresses all took advantage of this haven for the moderate charge of one pound, ten shillings, a week. Betty Boothroyd, a past Speaker of the House of Commons, recently recorded that she stayed at the club when she was a Tiller Girl.

Greek Street has long been frequented by 'ladies of the night', and it struck the girls as quite amusing for the club to be situated in the centre of such a notorious area of London. Everyone was aware that the common-room windows overlooked the street where various interesting happenings could be observed. Our favourite occupation was to watch the women standing under the street-lamps, waiting for customers. When a woman was successful and disappeared into her flat, we would time how long the man was inside. We also recorded the number of men, who, in the course of an hour, patronised each woman. For most of us, it was our first glimpse of the wicked world and certainly an eye-opener.

Largely, I was lucky with accommodation and usually made very welcome wherever I stayed. But earlier in the century, standards seem to have been pretty grim by all accounts and it was mostly comedians who saw humour in adverse conditions. An artiste by the name of Will Wise, wrote a poem, entitled, "The Pro's Lament", which included the following verse:-

"Seek a cosy combined, furnished in old-fashioned grace;
A picture of Randle, a po with no handle,
And two ruptured ducks in a case.
The landlady's plump, with two chins and a hump,
And about her late husband she bleats;
She tells you with tears she's been letting for years,
And you know that its true by the sheets...."

The comedian, Arthur Askey, told an amusing story on this theme. One landlady asked him what he liked to eat - and did he like cheese. Arthur said cheese was O.K., and he received cheese in various guises for every meal. One morning, the landlady came into his room to tend the fire, and upon seeing some soot dangling from the grate, cried, "Oh look, there's a stranger on the hearth!" whereupon Arthur replied, caustically, "I hope its the butcher!"

Stories about the escapades of "The Crazy Gang" were constantly being circulated in the theatre world. "The Crazy Gang" played in London's West End for many years and consisted of the comedians, Nervo & Knox, Naughton & Gold, and 'Monsieur' Eddie Gray. They got up to all kinds of mischief and once stood round a letter-box in a busy London street, while one of them peered into the slit, enquiring, "And how long did you say you have been in there?" A crowd of people soon gathered round the letter-box - the cue for the 'Gang' to slip away.

Islands are said to be fortunate for people born under the sign of Libra and I can confirm the veracity of this opinion. Holyhead is an unlikely town for a summer show. It is more of a port than a holiday resort, but nevertheless, holiday-makers came from all parts of Anglesey to see it, and we played to full houses.

The show, entitled, "Rendezvous" was situated at the Town Hall, Holyhead. This building had a drab, uninspiring exterior composed of cream-coloured bricks (another loo!), but held a large hall, a balcony, and an imposing stage graced with red velvet curtains, upon which the Welsh Dragon was embroidered in gold.

The producer, one Kewans Christie, also sang in a fine bass-baritone voice, and John Baskcomb, the comedian in the show, was the great-grandson of J.W. Baskcomb, a famous actor in his day.

It was decided very early in the season that my act would follow John's. This was his own idea, as he remarked, "I would prefer to *precede* your act, Pat, rather than follow it." Praise, indeed!

When I first entered the Town Hall a decorator was whistling, "Hear my song, Violetta", a song I featured in my act, so I took that as a good omen, which it proved to be. The great Irish tenor, Josef Locke, sang this number, and once, while rehearsing for pantomime at the Empire Theatre, Oldham, Locke was playing there to packed houses. I would often slip into the theatre to hear that marvellous pure voice, which he combined with an electrifying personality and stage presence. I was dubious about working the same song the week following Josef Locke's appearance, and confided my fears to the producer. "Nonsense!", he cried. "You have a good voice, so keep it in." I took the advice, and even though I followed in the steps of a great singer, my fears were unfounded.

The company at Holyhead received an invitation to board the Trinity House boat, 'Patricia', so of course I had to have a picture of the ship and the signatures of all the officers. I was asked to sing for them, and then we played silly games. One game began with someone saying, "I, Mary, having no sons, how many sons hast thou O'.........?" (pointing to another person). Each time, an extra word was added to the sentence and the number of 'sons' also increased. If mistakes occurred, the faces of the culprits were marked with circles of blackened cork. I decided to avoid the cork marks by carefully remembering each verse. It was great fun and the officers were charming men.

Forty-three years later, while watching the Commemoration Of D-Day on television, the commentator, during the flotilla review, exclaimed, "And there is the Trinity House boat, Patricia,' which was one of the ships that took part in active service during the last war." I was thrilled, and it brought the memories flooding back.

John Baskcomb said it would be fun to hire a sailing dinghy for a sea trip, and as he had been a lieutenant-commander in the navy during the 2nd World War, I thought he would 'know his onions', so to speak. It was the first time I had been sailing and I found it to be a glorious feeling; whipping through the waves with the wind at our backs. My parents would have had ten thousand fits had they known, because I could not swim a stroke and there were no life-belts on board. We sailed regularly, keeping inside the long jetty wall that stretched out to sea. The man who was responsible for the building of it, committed suicide by jumping off the end of it. I would have thought that there were cheaper and less time-consuming ways of ending one's life.

One afternoon, we took Kewans with us, and that day everything went badly wrong. The brisk wind that took us out, suddenly dropped, and we were becalmed. We also noticed that we were in the grip of a very strong current that was taking us out into the Irish Sea! The boat, bobbing in the open sea, seemed even smaller, now, and Kewans started to sing, "Down among the dead men let us lie", until we told him to shut up and think what to do. But there was little we *could* do in the circumstances.

My companions tried rowing against the current but it was an impossible task. A speed boat shot past leading a huge wash in its wake, and to avoid being capsized, John employed the oars and turned the boat so that we went *through* the wash -it felt like being in a cockleshell. Things were looking very grim indeed, when we spied the Holyhead life-boat coming our way, and yes, they had seen our plight. We were towed, ignominiously but very thankfully, back to the shore.

Once, we sailed into the inner harbour, where sailors on a destroyer threw boxes of Dairy Milk chocolates into our boat. I had no fear of the sea, but now I look back and wonder at my recklessness.

A group of us from the show went to Llandudno for the day, and in the evening looked in at a dance hall. The manager recognised us and asked if John and I would join him in adjudicating the Beauty Contest and choose Miss Llandudno, 1951. Artistes are familiar with this type of request. It is all part of life's rich pattern!

When the season ended, none of us wanted to leave the island, so we decided to split into two groups of four and try for some cabaret work. Joan Parry, the pianist, played for one group, while I accompanied the artistes in my group. We had posters printed and soon obtained an extra month's engagements in unusual and interesting venues.

One of them was a tiny church hall in the middle of nowhere. We could not imagine anyone turning up for the show, and in the late afternoon we had tea at a farmhouse. Spread upon a snow-white tablecloth, the meal consisted of brown eggs, home-made jam and cream, lovely crunchy bread with butter, and copious amounts of tea which we drank from delicate, bone-china tea-cups. It was delicious, and I believe it cost only sixpence each!

Back at the hall, people were already drifting in. They must have walked there, or flown on broomsticks, as no vehicles were parked outside.

Eventually, it really *was* time to leave Anglesey and what for me, had been a truly magical island. At that time, I had no hint that other 'magical' islands were in store!

In the Spring of 1952 I became leading lady in the revue, "Nightbirds", produced by Frank O'Brian and Janice Hart. The costumes were extremely lavish and in one scene as 'Lady Hamilton', I wore a sumptuous black-velvet gown and all the diamante I could accommodate.

I opened the scene with a song extolling the exploits of Lord Nelson, then the curtains opened to reveal a huge sailing hip, a company of sailors, and of course, 'Horatio' himself. In another part of the show I featured that beautiful song, "The barcarolle" from the "Tales of Hoffman", and wore a long, ivory satin, medieval gown - it was quite gorgeous.

At the Palace Theatre, Grimsby, the patrons occupying front seats in the stalls, suddenly got up and walked out in the middle of my solo spot. "I must be rotten for the audience to leave the theatre," I thought, and could not wait to get off the stage. But the unforeseen had occurred. The sea had actually entered the theatre and most of the seating was awash! The orchestra pit was also inundated; the musicians continuing to play with the water swirling round their knees!

The town of Grimsby is situated on the estuary of the river Humber and is famous for its port and docklands. The Palace Theatre, standing near the docks, had suffered from an exceptionally high tide, but the irony of a flood occurring during a show which featured a naval scene, did not escape the audience. The laugh was on us!

My parents came to see the show at York, and my father commented, "All that jewellery will suit our Pat down to the ground." A Yorkshire way of saying that I enjoyed wearing the costumes.

In "Nightbirds", there was a certain air of formality between the management and the artistes. I was always addressed as 'Miss Dawson', which I thought was rather nice. I also thought that Frank O'Brian was 'rather nice', too, and would hang on to everything he said - gazing at him with moonstruck eyes. He was not a young man, but he was well preserved, and his manner was charming - quiet and gentle. He once said to me, "You know, Miss Dawson, one day a knight in shining armour will come and carry you off," and he touched my cheek, smiling, mischievously. He must have known I was rather 'gone' on him, and that was me put in my place - though very kindly.

I had excruciating toothache during that tour, and plucking up my courage, had two large molars, removed. The following week at Birmingham, however, I woke one morning to find that I had haemorrhaged all over the pillow, so my landlady sent me to the Dental Hospital. There, they discovered that the dentist had made a complete mess of the extractions. So much for being brave! There were splinters of bone in the flesh, which was rapidly turning septic, so they had to clean the large cavity down to the jawbone (the extracted teeth had been adjacent ones). The hole was then plugged with gauze dipped in antiseptic.

By curtain-up time I looked like a chipmunk and had difficulty in forming words, as saliva continuously gathered in my mouth. Throughout the 'Barcarolle' number the first violinist was sprayed with a haze of fine moisture which glistened in the spotlight, and if nothing else, gave the correct atmosphere to the song.

The revue mostly played No.1 dates, i.e. Moss and Stoll theatres, and among other artistes, featured an adagio act comprising of two men and a girl. A huge rope web covered the back of the stage, the men dressed as spiders, with the girl as the fly. Typical of this kind of act, the female was small and slim, so that she could be thrown easily by the strong, muscular men - the bearers. They used her as a skipping-rope and swung her around by an arm and a leg, and finally they threw her onto the 'web', to which she clung, struggling. The 'fly' was caught.

It was a very good act, but these people kept a fox in their room which lived in a wooden box. I took it for a walk in Newcastle-upon-Tyne, and the poor thing pulled on its lead the whole time. I often wish I had let it go that day.

I was shown newspaper photographs, taken with the animal. The fox was obviously kept as a publicity gimmick. It worried me a lot to think of the creature living in such poor conditions, and the smell was quite strong, too. Not the nicest aroma to have in one's bedroom, I would have thought.

Sometimes, I was in the same accommodation as this act, and one night I heard the fox scratching and whining for what seemed like hours. Suddenly, there was a loud bang, followed by silence. I dread to think what had happened. Perhaps the poor thing had been hit on the head with something and killed, because I never saw it again. If the fox had been killed it must have been quick as both those men were very strong, but the episode haunted me for months. Nowadays, I am a strong supporter of charities which fight against cruelty to animals. I look back and curse my stupidity in failing to report that case to the R.S.P.C.A. What fools we mortals be. I worked with many stars in the theatre. One of them, Jill Summers, was a very funny comedienne who would eventually join the cast of "Coronation Street", as 'Phyllis'. Jill paid me a great compliment when she remarked, in my presence, to a theatre manager, "We could do with a lot more artistes like Pat, you know."

One of my Principal Girls in pantomime, was a Scottish soubrette, Mary Lee. We had great fun and lots of laughs during the run. Mary called me the 'Big Yun', while she was the Wee

Yun'. In Manchester we went to see Max Bygraves at the Palace Theatre. Mary had worked with him in Scotland, and after the matinee we made our way to his dressing-room. Max made us a pot of tea while we chattered about show business, and before we left, he gave me a signed photograph of himself. A really charming man.

At the Theatre Royal in Stockport, I met Mrs. George Formby, Senior - the mother of the ukulele-playing star. She was living in a small caravan behind the theatre, and one day I knocked on the door to ask for an autograph. She received me, kindly, but it was very difficult to believe that this old lady, the mother of one of Britain's biggest stars of stage and screen, called that obscure caravan, standing on a piece of waste ground, 'home'.

Salford Hippodrome was situated in a grim, squalid part of Manchester, where the houses looked as though they had been dipped in bags of soot. That week, I stayed at a large, dismal public house, a good twenty minutes walk from the theatre. One of the girls from our company invited me to her birthday party, to be held after the show, and I accepted the invitation. Around midnight, I tried to ring for a taxi to take me back to my lodgings, but the line was dead, I would have to walk back.

It was pouring 'cats and dogs' and I felt rather apprehensive as I trudged through the gloomy and deserted streets. I worried about the hotel, too, it must have closed ages ago. I reached the forbidding building, and of course, the door was locked and there were no lights showing. When the bell failed to summon a response, I banged on the door, but everything remained silent, and I was now wet through. I envisaged having to sit on the doorstep all night.

Then the headlights of a vehicle illumined the darkness, and most probably me, looking like 'Little Nell'. The car, slowed,

then stopped. Why had it stopped? Alarm bells rang in my head, until I recognised a police car. The driver got out and asked me what my problem was. I explained the situation and the officer, grinned, "Well now, we can't have you outside on such a rotten night, can we?" I agreed, we could not, whereupon he hammered hard upon the door, "That should wake 'em up," and it did! A light was switched on, and the bolts, drawn. I thanked the policeman and apologised to the tousle-haired proprietor, who was not well pleased at being so rudely awakened from his slumbers. The next time I played that theatre, I stayed in a cosy little house with a nice, motherly lady who could not do enough for me. Some, you win!

Chapter 3
Romance & Rodents

1953 saw me in another revue - a show bursting with talent. A young coloured girl - an acrobatic-contortionist, featured the then famous "Tassel Dance". This involved manoeuvring her body so that the tassels, placed strategically on her bra, rotated at an alarming rate.

One artiste in "Follies Montmartre" was petulant and highly strung. She took violent likes and dislikes to other people in the show, and when she declared that she 'liked' one of the females, the person in question was requested to share her dressing-room. (Her influence in this matter was entirely dependent upon the pulling-power of her act.)

Her 'friendships' invariably ended after a week or two, and we would laugh and remark to each other, "Its *your* turn, next." My own 'turn' also arrived, but I did not find it particularly awkward as most of the time the lady was absent from the dressing-room. I think I lasted three weeks!

In this production, and apart from my own speciality act, I joined with three other artistes, Syd England, Johnnie Heyward and Alan Fielding (a teenager with an exceptionally pure voice), to form a very strong vocal quartet, "The Millionaires". When the curtains opened, the scenery depicted the East End of London with the four of us dressed in ragged clothes and seated on orange boxes round an old fire bucket. (A lifestyle still in evidence in the present day!)

"The Millionaires" always brought the house down. We sang popular ballads, both singly and in unison, and we 'gelled' pretty well off-stage which is always a bonus when you have to work together.

Syd was a great sport. He called me "The Duchess", because when I walked out I usually wore a smart black suit, high-heeled shoes, a large black hat trimmed with yellow roses, and carried a walking umbrella. I saw the delicious hat in a milliners shop in Preston and could not resist it. Thus arrayed, I would sally forth, feeling rather grand.

Despite having friends in different shows, I ploughed a lonely furrow and up to the age of 26, never had a boy friend. I really was a very late starter, but things were about to change in that area of my life.

At Hulme Hippodrome in Manchester, my parents arrived to see the show, and afterwards, came to my dressing-room. It was a lovely room, all pink and gold, with drapes, velvet chairs, and lots of lighting. It was very similar to Joy Hayden's dressing-room at the Lyceum Theatre, which I had admired all those years ago.

While I was entertaining my parents, Robin, another act in the show came along with a message. When he had gone, my father said, "He looks a nice young man. Why don't you have a chat with him?" I thought this was a strange remark, coming from my father and in view of his earlier strictures concerning the opposite sex, so I just laughed. However, one way or another, our paths eventually crossed and we started going out for coffee together and attending matinees at the cinema.

Robin was six foot tall, with dark hair and grey eyes, and offstage always wore glasses. One day, he took them off, and when I saw him without these appendages, he looked so handsome that I fell in love with him, there and then. By the time the show arrived at Collins Music Hall in London, we were both on cloud nine! Incidentally, playing Collins Music Hall was very important to me, as most of the great artistes of yesteryear had trod those boards. Collins had seen the very best.

Robin and I never actually lived together, but we arranged to stay in the same accommodation each week, in separate rooms. Who were we trying to kid?

In London, the young son of the landlady told us of his interest in the Occult. He produced a Ouija board and we tried it out with him. The messages we received were very unusual. The gist of them being that there was a burial pit just behind Collins Music Hall, and a spirit coming through the board, stated that she was one of the people who were buried there.

She said it was a plague pit and was very worried because there had been talk of digging it up to lay the foundations of a new building. She told us that her name was Mary and that she had been only thirteen years old when she died of the plague. Well, all this was most mysterious, so we made enquiries at the theatre, and sure enough, the spirit of 'Mary' was correct. There was a burial pit behind the theatre, and plans had been laid to clear it for building purposes. However, the remains of those buried there were to be moved to consecrated ground.

The manager of the theatre showed us a skull, unearthed some years previously, which he always kept on his desk! So, we held another session on the board and explained things to 'Mary'. She was much cheered by our words and thankful that her bones would be laid to rest in a proper grave.

On a happier note, when the show played Liverpool, the management asked Robin and I if we would entertain at Burtonwood, the American Forces Camp, along with the Tassel Dancer. Two cabaret spots were required, and Louis Preager and his Orchestra would be in attendance. Burtonwood lay outside Warrington and was not far from the show's next venue, so at the expense of a quiet Sunday (extra cash always being useful), we agreed.

Everything was laid on for the G.I's, and the food was out of this world. I particularly noticed the long dishes of fresh strawberries piled high with cream, nuts, and goodness knows what else. There was a proper 'cabaret' atmosphere, too, with I tables round the dance-floor, spotlights, etc:

Louis Preager said not to worry about the dots (band parts), as the boys would follow me. They really 'went to town' with 12th Street Rag" and were with me all the way. I had been informed that the troops preferred 'pop' numbers to classics, so as always, I followed instructions and gave them what they wanted.

My frequent allusions to the above mentioned 'Rag' may give the impression that it was the only piece I played! Happily, such was not the case. My repertoire included such classics as "The Sabre Dance", "The Flight of the Bumble Bee", and "Dance of the Hours".

The love affair with Robin, continued. After retiring for the night, we would sneak into each other's rooms. Sexually, I had been 'awakened' and discovered that being 'in love' evoked a sensuality which constantly surprised me. It had been worth waiting for.

Looking back from the 90's and its 'anything goes' attitude to sex, our behaviour seems extremely prudish. But the moral code in those days was very different from the so-called sexual liberation of today, in which the word, 'love' is hardly ever mentioned.

In Belfast, I crept into Robin's room where the rays of a Full Moon filled it with a soft light. Then, horror of horrors, we heard footsteps on the stairs, followed by a tap on the door and the landlady's head appearing round it. "I just wanted to tell you that we're having a wee hoolie in the kitchen," said she. "Just in case ye think its a bit noisy." She batted not an eyelid and was gone. A 'hoolie' is an Irish party, and soon we heard sounds of merriment rising from the lower regions of the house. There was not a little in the bedroom, as after the initial shock we screeched with mirth. I was sure that I would only be thought of as a 'fast woman'.

Robin, frequently and expertly impersonated people, and he was soon taking-off the landlady's sister who was always betting on horses and losing her money - or so she said. She moaned continually in heavy Irish accents, "Do you know, I put five pounds on a dead cert, and I haven't got a penny left." This, while helping herself to another whiskey. As we heard the same story every day her comments started to wear a bit thin. When Robin mimicked her in private, however, it was highly entertaining.

On tour, you always found that audiences in a particular theatre had a preference, say, for comedy, while singers were favoured in another city. So, before an artiste set foot on the stage of a theatre, they knew who was most likely to walk away with the honours, that week.

A case in point was the comedian in the above-mentioned revue. His sketches and comedy routines were unique and entirely his own material. Initially, he found fame at the Windmill Theatre in London. This was a notorious venue for comedians because apart from the comedy spot, the show consisted of beautiful half-naked girls in exotic costumes.

The Windmill was known in the business as the comedian's grave-yard, because the type of audience it attracted was usually men in raincoats! Be that as it may, quite a few comedians who appeared there went on to become household names, and our top-of-the-bill was one of them. His comedy was brilliant, dry and witty, and all went well until we played the Empire Theatre, Belfast, where the patrons sat in stoney silence. However, he still had to perform twice nightly with the knowledge that he was going to 'die' on stage. Not a pleasant prospect.

We all felt terribly sad for him, but there was absolutely nothing to be done, and by the end of the second week (the Empire held shows over for two weeks), he had given in his notice. In my opinion, this was a very silly thing to do as he had them roaring with laughter everywhere else and Belfast was only a bad memory.

When we left Northern Ireland, late, one Saturday night, the docks were lined with the dark shapes of youths, shouting, "Get back to the boat! Get back to yer own country!" Apparently, this was a regular occurrence every time a boat left Belfast harbour, but we were nothing loathe to obey the hostile commands.

A replacement comedian had to be found for the show and came in the shape of Charlie Ellis - 'A Broth of a Boy', as his billing proclaimed. Charlie was another first-rate artiste whom I was to meet again, some years later.

When the show ended its long run, my relationship with Robin continued, although we were separated for the time being. I went to the Savoy Theatre, Clacton-on-Sea, in a summer show for Elkan and Barry Simons; appropriately, if a trifle obviously entitled, "Savoy Ahoy!" Robin, meanwhile, toured in Variety, but he managed to come to Clacton, once or twice, where he was welcomed with open arms. I really missed him, dreadfully.

Autumn, found us in a short, pre-pantomime revue, touring in London. It was about this time that both our sets of parents put their feet down in no uncertain manner. I had met Robin's folk on two or three occasions and they seemed perfectly amicable. Perhaps they thought it was just a fling for Robin, as now it seemed there was no chance of our getting engaged -it was out of the question.

My own parents said much the same things, because, "My boy friend did not earn enough to keep me in the manner to which I was accustomed." Perhaps they imagined us starving in a garret! Of course, it was a lot of balderdash, but at the time it was a serious matter and very upsetting.

The arguments went on and on, and when the tour ended, what proved to be our final parting took place on Bedford station. Although there were the usual protestations of undying love, which on my part at least, came from the heart, deep down I knew we would never meet again.

At home, there were many tearful scenes, and I fought hard against my parents' wishes - after all, I was 27 years of age at the time! Doubts about Robin's feelings for me kept me awake at night. Had he grown tired of me? Was there someone else? Was it all his parents' doing? Fear of rejection stopped me from going to see him. I knew I could not bear that. I would rather keep on hoping that things would come right, eventually.

There really was no time to fall apart, either, as pantomime beckoned and I was off again to attend rehearsals. Unless you are together in a double act, the stage is one of the best careers for keeping couples separated. And although I was still deeply in love with Robin, circumstances still kept us apart. It was to be another eighteen months before I would meet the man I was destined to marry, but at the time, I felt my life had ended.

After the panto season, I was booked for a new revue which ran throughout 1955. Denise Vane was one of the Principals in the show and invited me into her dressing-room where she offered me a glass of whiskey. She always looked so cool, charming and in complete control. But after that drink, such was not the case with me. I performed on stage in a dreamlike haze - a most uncomfortable feeling and one which I vowed never to repeat.

At the Grand Theatre, Southampton, Denise explained that she had been invited out for a meal by one of her admirers, and would I accompany her, as she said there was safety in numbers.

So, after the show, we were duly conducted into an Austin Healey convertible by a plump little man and whisked off into the night at great speed. He may have been somewhat disappointed at my appearance on the scene but gave us a sumptuous meal in a country hotel and delivered us safely back to our accommodation.

That particular week Denise and I were staying at the same address. I occupied a room in which I ate and slept (known in the profession as a combined chat!). This room was on the ground floor next to the kitchen and one night, after supper, I had retired to bed with a favourite book when a sudden scrabbling noise under the nearby table, made me lift the tablecloth and peer beneath it. The landlady had a sweet spaniel puppy and I thought it must have got into the room. What I actually saw made me freeze. A large grey rat was sitting there, wiping his whiskers!

My limbs would not move, but after the shock wore off a little, I stood up on the bed and knocked on the ceiling, as I knew that Denise occupied the room above my own. Nothing happened. Then, the rat slowly hopped towards an easy chair in a corner of the room and disappeared beneath it.

Realising that my S.O.S. had been in vain, I stepped quietly onto the table walked across it, and descended via a chair to the floor, where I made a quick exit from the room.

I woke the landlady who sent her husband and another man (the electrician from the theatre), to find the rat. Bangs and thuds were heard, then the sound of breaking glass, followed by silence. I went downstairs and gingerly pushed open the door. "Have you found it?" I asked. The electrician grinned, "Yes, you're standing on it." I sprang back as he lifted a newspaper that covered the corpse. The rat had led them a merry dance, and the window had been broken in the process. I flatly refused to occupy the room again, so the electrician obligingly allowed me to use his, while he slept in the 'rat' room with the broken window.

My adventure found its way into "*The Stage*" newspaper, in a column written by James Hartley and headed 'Presence of Mind'. But, had this incident occurred during the last twenty-five years, things would have been very different. I would not have stood by while that creature was killed. Some means would have been found to release it, unharmed. It is a good example of the way in which I have 'grown' over the years, and how my innate compassion and love for all living creatures eventually manifested.

At the Metropolitan Theatre in London (affectionately known as the 'Met'), Annette Gaye, a young lady in the show, popped into my dressing-room with a request. It arose when she and her husband, Noel, were in the theatre bar. An old gentleman approached them and asked Noel if he would allow Miss Gaye, and a friend of her choice, to have dinner with him. He explained that he was a very lonely man and that it would give him great pleasure to entertain Annette and a friend. Noel had agreed, providing I went with her, so it was arranged for the following evening.

After the show, we both put on our glad rags and sallied forth, but we blinked and stared at each other when we saw a Rolls Royce glide up to the Stage Door. Could this car be for us? The chauffer saluted us and opened a rear door. After making sure that our host was indeed in the vehicle, we sank into the luxury of the Queen of automobiles as it slid away from the kerb.

Our host informed us that we were to have dinner at the 'White Bear' restaurant in Piccadilly - and so we did! I cannot remember the gentleman's name so I will call him 'Cedric' - he looked like a 'Cedric'.

The 'White Bear' was an elegant establishment for the well-to-do, and during the meal a gypsy violinist came to our table and serenaded us with the strains of a love song. Cedric was on excellent raconteur and regaled us with amusing stories.

He also explained that his wife had died some years before, and said that he really enjoyed taking out pretty ladies from the theatre, now and then. It seemed we were not the first females to encounter his generosity.

Speeding back through the darkened city, we came first to Annette's accommodation. She thanked him, prettily, and departed, and I realised that I was alone in a car with two men who were virtually strangers. After a moment's panic, the Rolls stopped again, and it was my turn to leave. I thanked Cedric, sincerely, for what had been a very special evening, then he was gone, and I never saw him again. I often wondered who he was - obviously a very rich man, indeed. He had not volunteered any information of a personal nature, and we were too good mannered to enquire.

The following week we were due to play the Theatre Royal in Barnsley, but a train-strike was planned for the week-end, so the management urged me to order a taxi straight after my act on the Saturday, and grab a train to Sheffield. "That way," they said, "you should make it, and it will be one less worry for us."

I caught what must have been the last train to Liverpool, via Sheffield but by the time we reached Derby, it was well past midnight - the time for the strike. There was a long and ominous wait at Derby station, during which the passengers fidgeted and wondered what was going to happen. I was just going to jump up and find out, when the ticket collector appeared and informed us that in spite of the time, they were willing to take the train to its destination at Liverpool. He looked as though he expected a round of applause for his statement, but merely received noncommittal stares for his pains. I would soon see the welcoming word, 'SHEFFIELD', on a station platform and gave a tired sigh of relief. It was great to be going home.

We endured a very dreary week at the theatre in Barnsley and counted the days until the final performance. There could be no greater contrast between the packed houses, the ambience, and the excellent orchestra at the 'Met', and the draughty, half-empty theatre of the mining town. The 'orchestra' consisted of only five musicians, who were all 'at sea' when I played "The Sabre Dance". But the most unheard of thing to occur in any theatre worthy of the name, was when the drummer departed half-an-hour before the end of the show, in order to catch his last bus. And this was standard procedure! Too bad for the artistes billed late in the show, especially if they relied upon the percussion section of the orchestra! It was difficult to believe that this was the same revue that had 'wowed' them at the 'Met', the previous week.

After Barnsley there was a week-out, and as most of the company had not seen their homes for almost a year, everyone looked forward to the rest, and to recovering from the stress of Barnsley, too!

A telegram arrived asking if I could return to the 'Met' that same week. I knew such a speedy return to a theatre was quite an honour - especially a London theatre, but I was sorely in need of a rest, so I thanked them for thinking of me and forwarded my apologies. I was very sad, some years later, when the Metropolitan, like so many other theatres, was demolished to make way for a concrete monstrosity.

There were times in that same revue, when I was desperately unhappy and longed to leave. The cause of this was another speciality act, a man who was attractive neither in manner or appearance, and whom I will call, 'Frank'.

It all started when Frank asked me to go to the cinema with him, and I gave some excuse not to go. From that moment, he began a hate campaign against me and sometimes even attempted to spoil my act in some way. He would also stand in the position I occupied in the finale line-up, just prior to the curtains opening. It was all done to annoy me, and there were dozens of other petty, but disturbing incidents of a similar nature.

In Ipswich, some of the company, including myself, were staying at the same hotel, and Frank announced, in front of Denise and others, that should I vacate my bedroom and allow Denise to occupy it, as she had nowhere to stay. I pointed out that I had booked the room well in advance and that if Frank was a gentleman, he was the one to oblige Denise by vacating his room. Denise waved the matter aside, and said I was not to upset myself. She knew that Frank was getting at me.

I hated all the angst coming from this man, so I rang Dick Ray in London, whose production it was. However, Dick said that he wanted both our acts to remain in the show, and tried to console me with the usual platitudes, saying it would soon blow over, etc:

Actually, things got much worse, and one night when my tormentor came to my dressing-room with some made-up tale, I suddenly, and quite literally, 'saw red'. A ruddy haze formed in front of my eyes, and I grabbed the nearest thing, which happened to be an umbrella, and whacked Frank repeatedly over the head with it. He backed away and made a swift exit, but I was shaking all over, and went to see Dick Montague (the principal comedian and acting-manager of the show for Dick Ray). I asked him to do something immediately about the situation, as I wanted, out. Dick could see that I was practically in tears, and said he would speak to Frank, forthwith. After that, things were easier for a week or so.

Alas, it soon started over again, with Frank leering at me from the wings while I was on stage and performing other unpleasant tricks he had thought up. So much so, that when we reached

Newcastle-upon-Tyne, I went to the police station and made a complaint against the man.

I explained everything to the patient officer, saying I could not work properly with Frank's interference. In short, I said that I wanted his machinations to cease.

A plain-clothes policeman was sent round to the theatre, and I learned that he had spoken to Frank about my complaint. Frank, however, attempted to turn the tables by saying it was I who had caused the trouble because he, Frank, had refused to take me out. The nerve of the man!

The policeman accompanied me to my hotel and explained that beyond giving Frank a warning, there was nothing that the police could do, as he had not caused me any actual bodily harm. I could not believe what occurred next. The policeman saw me safely inside the hotel, then *made a pass at me!* I gave him his marching orders and wondered what on earth I had done to deserve such treatment. For a member of the Police Force of whom I had requested aid, to betray his calling by asking me for a kiss, was completely incomprehensible. Had he believed Frank's story? In such a situation, was a man more readily believed than a woman? That night I cried myself to sleep and dreaded waking up the next day. As for going to the theatre ...

Soon after this, Raymond, one of Dick Ray's sons, arrived on the scene, no doubt sent by his father to sort things out. He approached me one morning and said that Frank would like to apologise for his behaviour. And would I accept a small gift as compensation? Raymond added, "I think he means it, Pat, so do take the gift." Oh, to be free from that heavy cloud of apprehension every time I entered the Stage Door! I agreed to accept the apology, whereupon Raymond beckoned to Frank who was lurking in the corridor, and we shook hands on it. I am pleased to say that he never bothered me again. Perhaps calling in the police had something to do with it, after all.

At the Empire Theatre, Portsmouth, Dick Ray asked me to play the role of Principal Boy in his pantomime, to be staged at that theatre. I was to be 'Robin Hood' in "Red Riding Hood", and a contract was drawn up forthwith. Speaking to Dick, face to face, I told him exactly what I had been through with Frank and enquired if *he* had a role in the pantomime. Dick smiled, patted my shoulder, and replied that Frank *would* have a part - he was to play the 'Wolf'! I complimented Dick on his casting abilities and learned that as 'Robin Hood' I would have to enact a sword fight with the 'Wolf'.

Dick also mentioned that he had once promised Frank's father he would keep an eye on his son, and help him as much as he could. It seemed that Frank had always been withdrawn and often blamed other people for the negative traits in his own personality. Dick said, I was not to worry, as he, and his wife, Cissie, would be on hand throughout the run. There would be no nonsense, as he had already spoken to Frank about the matter.

Dick Ray was the uncle of the famous star, Peter Sellers. Dick's wife, Cissie, being the sister of Peg, Peter's mother. Their large family had been connected with show business for a very long time, going back to Seller's maternal grandmother, Welcome Mendoza, who had belonged to the Sephardic Jewish Community. As far back as the 17th century, Oliver Cromwell had given these people permission to make London their home, and to establish a burial site there.

Welcome, soon formed a touring variety company and adopted the stage name of Miss Belle Ray. After her marriage, she eventually gave the control of her registered London company, to her sons. Thus, the Ray Bros. Productions Ltd., came into being in 1925 - one of them being my employer, Dick Ray.

Building to many touring shows, the business was brought under the aegis of Moss' Empires Ltd., which owned a chain of theatres regularly housing the Ray Bros, revues. And beside all this, Dick Ray, Cissie, and a brother, Ray Ray, owned Ray Studios and Burls Stage Draperies, which supplied scenery, stage curtains and costumes to the theatrical profession.

Dick's two sons, Dick Ray Jr, and Raymond Ray, were handsome young men, and always on hand to help their father. Raymond travelled with revues, and his elder brother finally went to Jersey where he organised cabarets and operated as an agent. Today, he is the owner of the Jersey Opera House, and Caesar's Palace.

While writing about the Ray family, Peter Sellers life story appeared on television, and I was suddenly confronted with a picture of Dick Ray in his younger days! An uncanny coincidence.

A unique stage effect called 'La Burl' was also shown on this programme. This entailed the projection of coloured slides into a pretty, scantily-clad female, who stood in front of a white screen on a darkened stage. To see it again after forty years was quite astonishing, and took me even deeper into the past.

' La Burl' was featured in the pantomime at Portsmouth, and during rehearsals I sat with Dick Ray in the stalls, watching a young lady transformed into a butterfly, a fairy queen, an Egyptian princess, and all manner of beautiful images. As one newspaper reporter put it, "A striptease act in reverse!" Dick was very proud of 'La Burl', and confided that he held the copyright of it, and had done so for many years. In a way, he was re-living the past and holding on to his memories through this tangible, phantasmagorical illusion.

It was thought to be Peter Seller's mother, Peg, who first introduced 'La Burl' to British audiences, when Peter was around one year old. Peg's act was named, 'Fire and the Woman', and built on Sir Henry Rider Haggard's famous book,

"She". Peg portrayed the priestess who bathed in the 'Flame of Eternal Youth' to attain immortality. She also appeared as various women in history, such as Joan of Arc and Cleopatra.

To return to "Red Riding Hood", Frank and I practised the sword fight routine, continuously, and his manner was always correct, even subservient. The hilt of my sword was decorated with gilt wire, and on the day of the dress rehearsal, a large blister formed on the palm of my hand, with a dark mark running up my arm. Arriving at the theatre, I bumped into the lady violinist from the orchestra, and showed my hand to her. "Good gracious!" she cried, "You must go immediately to the hospital, I think you have blood poisoning!" The wire on the hilt of the sword had caused a blister and infected my blood. The lady bundled me into a taxi and very kindly accompanied me to the hospital. After five injections, plus a poultice on my hand, I felt very groggy.

At the theatre, I donned my costume and thigh boots and stumbled onto the stage. I managed to run through my duet with Annette Gaye (Maid Marion), and the dance I had arranged for us, but found that playing the accordion in my speciality act, with a bulky bandage on my hand, was extremely difficult. And in the sword fight I used my good hand and wore a glove, as except for being left-handed when writing, I am ambidextrous. The next day we opened to a full house and I felt slightly better. I was informed that the sword fight looked very realistic from the front of house!

Dick asked me if I would tour in a new revue he was planning in the Spring of 1956. Along with the Empire Theatre, Portsmouth, it would play all the number one Moss Empire theatres, and he said he would particularly like me to play "The Sabre Dance" in my act. It sounded most encouraging, but it was not to be. Poor Dick died suddenly on New Year's Eve, and due to this sad event, my life changed, dramatically.

Dick's death cast a shadow upon the company, as although he had been an elderly man, he was always full of beans and well liked. The pantomime went on as usual of course, and there was also a Pantomime Ball at Southsea. My escort was Michael Rourke, the manager of the Empire Theatre, a tall, charming man from Shamrock Land. Notable guests included the Kaye Sisters who were appearing at Southsea.

Another late night excursion occurred when Jan Harding ('Simple Simon') and myself, were invited to do a 'spot' at an army camp on the Portsdown Hills, for a select party comprising of officers and their wives. I was not keen, as after two, three hour shows a day, plus many changes of costume, all I wanted was my bed. However, I agreed to go, and we set of for the hills in a chauffeur-driven car. Approaching the gates of the camp Jan played the fool by calling out, in Irish accents, that the I.R.A. had arrived!

Jan Harding was a very amusing man and kept us in hysterics off-stage. During rehearsals, there had been this thing about 'Charlie' and 'Dick', and when Jan brought it to our notice, we thought it was hilarious. Charles Meek was the Musical Director, while Dick Montague played the 'Dame' and also produced the pantomime, and it just seemed that whenever Dick wanted to speak to Charlie, ensconced in the orchestra pit, he was either filling his pipe, or had gone to the loo. So it went, "We'll take it from the introduction, Charlie - are you there, Charlie?" Whereupon, Charlie, if present, would reply, "Just coming, Dick," or, "Where did you say to start from, Dick?" and so on. It was just this silly thing, and the way Jan brought it to our notice, combined with the constant usage of the names, 'Charlie' and 'Dick', that seemed absurd and evoked so much mirth. We could also laugh at ourselves, if the occasion warranted it.

I never saw Jan's speciality act, as I was always changing when he was on stage, but I do remember hearing the song he finished on, "I wonder who's kissing her, now", which he sang in soft, yet very appealing tones.

People do not believe me when I tell them I was on a bill with so-and-so, but did not see their act. It does not occur to them that while an act is on stage, other artistes are busy changing for their next entrance. I missed Jan's act at the army camp, too, being dragged away to meet someone or other.

The Portsdown cabaret was the last late night and I was not sorry, as I did not feel one hundred per cent. The reason for this, revealed some months later, was more serious than I imagined at the time.

When the pantomime ended, I was requested to stay on in the same theatre for a week in Variety. I groaned at the prospect. Why, oh why, did I feel so tired all the time? And surely, the patrons of the Empire would appreciate a change after ten

weeks. However, I was reassured about this and persuaded to stay. So when the scenery was dismantled for another year; the wires from Eugene's Flying Ballet, retrieved, and the company had gone their separate ways, No.1 dressing-room was still occupied.

I sat alone for a while, nursing the bruises sustained from my fall the previous night (which I described earlier). What would I have given to have gone off with the others, who would soon be curled up in their own beds. Even my friend, the pony, who could count, and displayed his dexterity on the command of 'Five', 'Seven' or 'Ten', by either nodding his head or pawing the ground the required number of times, had long since departed. I missed him.

I slept solidly for the rest of Sunday and returned to the theatre for band-call on the Monday morning, where back-stage was full of strangers and bustle. Top of the Variety bill was Peter Sinclair - radio's 'Cock of the North', as his billing proclaimed. I sought him out and asked if he wished me to vacate No.1 dressing-room, which was now his by rights. He was quite charming about it, and exclaimed, "Ach no, lassie, keep it. I'll be right as rain in No.2," which I thought was really nice of him.

One night, the stalls were full of Japanese sailors who waved their arms about and shouted something like, "Ra, ra!" I thought I was getting 'the bird' until someone came back-stage and explained that this was how the Japanese showed their appreciation for an act. I wondered what they did to express their displeasure! One girl dissolved in tears when she came off-stage, until I hastily reassured her that all was well.

It reminded me of a club in Goldthorpe, a mining area in Yorkshire, where they played dominoes while you were on stage. They appeared not to notice you at all. At the end of your act, and providing they liked you, they would raise their arms instead of clapping, while you left the stage to the sound of your own footsteps. There was no prior warning of this strange custom, so it was quite demoralising for an artiste.

When I finally arrived home, my father, who had been ill for some time, was much worse, but his face brightened when he saw me, and I told him all my news. I was able to look after him and take some of the strain off my mother, who was as busy as ever. Dr. Billington's opinion of my father's health was extremely grave.

I saw the doctor on my own behalf, and he advised me to have a chest x-ray, forthwith. The results showed what they called a shadow on one lung, which was most probably the result of pneumonia some time in the past. This was true. I had been ill some years before, and remembered travelling to Manchester, very early one morning, in a freezing cold train.

I was on a Variety bill at the Theatre Royal, Stockport, and had to climb a steep hill in deep snow, to my accommodation. I found breathing difficult by the time I reached the top. It was cold in that house, too, and my bedroom had only linoleum on the floor, covered by a few small mats. I coughed throughout the night and developed chest pains, so the next day I bought some cough syrup which aided me, after a struggle, to bring up this brown-coloured mucus. One night, I must have passed out after my act, as I came round in the arms of a St. John's Ambulance man, who was waving smelling-salts under my nose. Everything about that week remains a horrible blur, but was most probably the cause of this chest trouble, although I was told there was no immediate cause for panic. There would be intermediate treatment prior to entering hospital for at least three months.

Chapter 4
Who is Arnold Crowther?

My father passed away on the 24th March, 1956, and in the midst of our sorrow, an aunt and uncle of mine rang to say that we should go and spend some time with them. They lived in Great Bookham, Surrey, and had this lovely bungalow with grounds that included an orchard, and everything was very peaceful at their abode. Then, one morning, I received a call from our neighbour in Sheffield, saying that a Robert Layton wanted me to ring him immediately. Layton was a theatrical agent in London, and I was curious to know what he wanted, so I got in touch. Robert told me there was a summer season for me in Shanklin, and hoped I was free to take the engagement. I explained that being unsure of my health, I was not contemplating any work in the near future. He sympathised, then said that the sea air would work wonders, and could I just meet the producer in Town? It was a difficult situation. I thought of my mother - she badly needed a rest from her employment. She was just not well enough to work after the shock of losing Father, so I decided to go to London.

Marjorie Ristori was a vivacious lady, who had trod the boards with her husband, Harry, for most of her life, and their summer show at Shanklin was in its 3rd year. Harry was a member of that elite theatrical order, the 'Water Rats', while Marjorie belonged to the distaff side as a 'Lady Ratling'. Over coffee, Marjorie explained that she had often seen my act in the London theatres, and could not believe her luck when Layton suggested me. So, finally I was signed to appear in 'Hilarity', at the Pier Casino, Shanklin.

When I told Uncle Norman the news, he exclaimed, "You're booked for 'Hilarity'? A good friend of mine is in that show, his name is Arnold Crowther". I laughed. "That's a coincidence. Who is Arnold Crowther?"

Uncle explained that he had known Crowther, a brilliant stage magician, for some time, as he belonged to Uncle's particular circle of friends and associates. Of course, I learned much later, when I had met Arnold, myself (the story of which I have told elsewhere), that he was deeply interested in real magic and the religious beliefs of ancient civilizations, including those of Britain and Egypt. He was particularly fascinated with Buddhism and owned a unique collection of curios from many parts of the world. Arnold often gave talks on these curios which included a shrunken head from the Jivaro tribe of South America and a death-pointing bone from the Aborigine race in Australia.

I talked to Arnold about my deep interest in the Feminine Principle - the divine Goddess who I knew, from what little I had read on the subject, was once worshipped as the 'Mother of All Living'. I was intrigued when he told me that She was still worshipped in the present day by people whom the world knew as witches, and who were organised in groups known as covens.

It was all extremely enthralling to me, and one day I stopped to look in the window of a bookshop, and immediately, my eyes were drawn to a book entitled, *"Witchcraft Today"*, by Gerald Gardner. I purchased it, forthwith. When I showed the book to Arnold his face lit up, "Why, Gerald is an old friend of mine I met him in London before the last war." Arnold was of the opinion that nothing occurs by accident, and he was sure that the Goddess had something planned for us in the future. How right he was!

Rehearsals for the show were very stressful, because after an evening's performance, we had to run through the next programme, and finally staggered off the pier around 3 a.m.! This practise continued until all five programmes were running. It was long before the days of Equity, an organisation formed to assist artistes and promote justice and fair play in their dealings with managements. Nowadays, robbing people of their sleep in order to further the production of a show, would simply not occur.

I shared accommodation with Gloria (a dancer in the show). Finding a place to stay was difficult because of the influx of holiday-makers. We moved three times before we were finally settled in a large house, just outside the town. It was chance that dictated sharing with Gloria, as we had little in common.

One morning, I woke up feeling quite ill, so stayed in bed while Gloria went off to the theatre. But suddenly, she reappeared, looking distraught. "Whatever's the matter?" I asked. "Oh dear, it's Arnold," she cried. "He asked me where you were, so I told him you had a cold." She looked behind her, fearfully, "He's coming to see you", she squeaked, her eyes the size of the proverbial saucers. It was my turn to look horrified. There was I, in bed, without any make-up, my hair in curlers, and feeling like death. "Oh, no, please tell him ....," but Gloria had fled.

Before I could even grab a comb, I heard muted voices in the hall, then the steady tread of feet on the stairs, followed by a knock on the door. Pulling up the sheets and shrinking into the pillows, I croaked, "Come in," and there was Arnold, looking quite concerned. "I'm sorry to disturb you, but I just had to see you when Gloria said you were ill." He smiled, "I have brought you something I hope you will like," and he put a parcel on the bed. "It arrived this morning from America."

My face was now as red as a beetroot, but I thanked him, warmly, thinking what a sight I must look. Arnold helped me to open the gift. It was an exquisite bust of Queen Nerfertiti, the wife of the heretic pharaoh, Akhanaton, and said to be the most beautiful woman in the world. Arnold's features, like those of the queen, betrayed no hint of emotion. "Why, it is quite lovely," I cried, "how very sweet of you." I held out my hand, but Arnold was halfway to the door. "Glad you like it. Get well soon." and he was gone.

Later in the season, when we were deeply in love, Arnold said that far from being put off by my appearance that morning, he was more attracted to me then ever! "I think the curlers did it," he grinned. Arnold's pet names for me were 'Funny Face' and 'Spider'!

We would walk to the 'Old Village' in Shanklin for coffee, or sit holding hands on a seat in Rylestone Gardens. We saw each other at every possible opportunity and continued our conversations. We used to frequent a cafe on the sea-front called 'The Golden Tortoise', and when we saw a little brass tortoise in an antique shop, Arnold bought it for me as a keepsake. It still stands on my mantelpiece, but 'Nerfertiti' holds pride of place.

Writing about one's life is a harrowing experience, as all the emotional times, both happy and sad, are lived through again, and the heart is filled with nostalgia and piquant memories. From what I have learned however, I am certain that future lives grant reunions with loved ones in yet more fascinating circumstances.

During that summer, my mother came to the island as she was feeling lonely and depressed without my father. She obtained employment in the Round Bar, adjoining the theatre. These buildings were owned by Mr. & Mrs. Henry Wood, the former, a retired sea captain. Mrs. Wood was a small, busy soul, who always dressed in nautical fashion and hailed everyone with a, "Hello my hearty!" or an optimistic, "Everything shipshape?"

A delightful cottage, owned by the Woods, was put at my mother's disposal, where nearly every day she provided me with a hot meal. Mother found that working in the Round Bar was very hard, and I worried about her, because although she looked younger than her sixty-five years, she had not fully recovered from my father's passing.

I informed her of my friendship with Arnold, and also introduced him to her. This was obviously the wrong thing to do at the time, as afterwards she exclaimed, "He's too old for you - he's old enough to be your father!" Now, Arnold *was* eighteen years older than me, but I could not see what that had to do with falling in love. He was also tall, dark and handsome with touches of silver at his temples, which bestowed a distinguished air.

I often wondered if my mother wanted me to remain single all my life, as no one seemed to be the right person for me. When the season ended, Arnold came to see me at home in Sheffield. He brought with him many wonderful curios he had collected during his travels, including a statue at least 3,000 years old. This represented the Ancient Egyptian deity - Isis, nursing her divine son, Horus. The Goddess had entered my home!

I suggested to Arnold, that as well as fulfilling his engagements in London, he might work in Sheffield, too, so that we could have more time together. His act was amazing, incorporating sleight-of-hand in the production of playing-cards, billiard-balls and lighted cigarettes. During the latter feat, one of the cigarettes was taken secretly into the mouth, via the tongue, and held there, until the appropriate moment, when it appeared between his lips - still lit! This always

brought gasps of astonishment from the audience. Arnold was also an expert in puppetry (he made over 500 puppets in his time), and all his many talents were combined with an excellent stage presence and a droll sense of humour.

I was sure that he would obtain engagements locally, and I was right. The first show he gave resulted in being offered more work than he could comfortably handle, so his date-book was filled well into the following year. Mother and I were in the audience that first night, and heard comments such as, "What an artiste!" and "He's a great act!", all in the best Yorkshire accents.

We learned that Arnold had been in Sheffield during the war with E.N.S.A., and had his own show entitled, "Black Magic". It included a Basuto choir, while Arnold performed the magic, hence the title. At a concert given for one of the steel works, the audience did not want the National Anthem to be played. This attitude resulted in Arnold striding onto the stage and announcing, "No God save the King1 - no show!" They got the message, and the anthem was duly played.

Arnold visited many theatres of war, and in Malta he met several acts who entertained as female impersonators. One, described himself as the 'Queen of Malta', having, as he put it, much influence with the top brass and others in authority!

Arnold was accepted by these effeminate men, or 'Gays', as they are called today, because he believed in live, and let live, and had no hang-ups regarding the sexual preferences of others. Here, I must stipulate, that although many female impersonators are definitely 'Gay', there are others who are not; it is merely a part of their act.

After the war, he was waiting on the platform at Bedford station, when a train pulled in. Soon, heads were popping out of windows, with effeminate voices crying, "Oh, look, there's Arnold!", and "Coo-ee, Arnold!" It was the touring company of the revue. "Soldiers in Skirts", and included many of the men whom he had met in Malta. Not in the least embarrassed by all this attention, Arnold grinned, and had a word with his wartime friends.

Sometimes, my mother would be scratchy with Arnold, and at others, as nice as pie. I think that deep down she liked him, but there was always that jealousy when she imagined he was taking me away from her. I talked it through with her on many occasions, but it was some time before she saw things from my point of view.

Like myself, Arnold was a Libran - and a true one. He was fair-minded, tolerant, and a fascinating raconteur. We would sit round the fire with mugs of hot tea, swopping stories about the most unsavoury 'digs' we had stayed in. Arnold's were hilarious. When he was in the Orkney's during the war his landlady would present him with a large piece of wood, upon which was tied a very small key. The house was part of a long terrace with the toilet situated at the end of the row. And as he strolled along, holding the piece of wood, neighbours, gossiping over fences, would call out, "Aye, ye'll find it at the end," or, "it's at the end of the brae.'

The toilet door was without hinges so one hand would be placed against it, to hold it in position. The toilet also lacked a roof, so when it rained Arnold was given an umbrella, and while nature took its course, his free hand held up the umbrella!

In Swindon, the toilet was at the top of the stairs, and when he occupied it, he would hear the sound of footsteps on the stairs, whereupon three pieces of toilet-paper were pushed under the door. Arnold calculated, one dirty wipe, one clean wipe, one polish!

Paper was scarce in wartime, and one landlady always said, "Be careful with the toilet-paper." So Arnold left a message on the wall of the smallest room, which read, "Due to the shortage of paper, will customers please use both sides!" A fellow artiste told him about a message in a house where he had stayed, and Arnold laughed and said, "Oh, I wrote that." There were more incongruous incidents when we travelled together. Arriving late in Coventry, we had to take the only accommodation available. It was really dreadful. The stairs and bedroom were bare of carpet, and the toilet was outside and also served as the dog's kennel - poor thing. For toilet-paper, square pieces of newspaper, hung on the wall.

The woman at this establishment was very ugly, almost bent double, and walked with the aid of a stick. She continually shouted at her pet budgie what presumably were meant to be terms of endearment, "Who's a booty? Who's a little treasure, then?" while banging the cage with her stick. Arnold whispered, " I know who is not a 'little booty'."

At the dinner table, we sat opposite 'the family', composed of said landlady, her husband, and their daughter - a young woman in her twenties. When I reached for the sauce, I was told, "No, that's not for you, its for the family." One night in that house was more than enough!

Our next visit to Coventry was in much more salubrious surroundings. We stayed at the Leofric Hotel and appeared on a television programme filmed at the same venue.

"Bid for Fame", was a series of programmes for aspiring artistes, and each week one act would be chosen to appear at a later date. This ultimately led to an outright winner who would gain a contract for more television appearances. Joe Loss and his Orchestra provided the music and the show was fronted by McDonald Hobley and Joan Edwards.

Most talent shows are fixed, as despite the viewers sending in their votes, the powers that be have already decided upon the winner. On this occasion we heard that a young woman with quite a small voice would win - and so she did! Nevertheless, we were very well received, and enjoyed the experience.

At the end of 1956, the Portsmouth pantomime went to Bedford, and I went with it. But finally, in the Spring of 1957 I entered a sanatorium in Sheffield for three months. This establishment had once been a large private house in its own grounds, and held some fifty patients. It stood in the Walkley district of the city, known as Commonside.

Everyone knew you had tuberculosis if you were admitted to 'Commonside'. I shared a room with two other patients, and the meals were enormous. We were urged to have second helpings of everything too, in order to build up our weight. It was six weeks before I put on any weight at all, then it slowly increased from seven stones, to just over eight stones.

You had to stay in bed and save your strength, so that your body could fight the disease. During those three months, I had two hundred injections of streptomycin, and when discharged, took a similar drug by mouth for a time.

The bookings that Arnold had obtained the previous year now came in handy, as he was able to visit me when he worked in Sheffield. He would walk up the steep hills to Commonside, as he hated buses, and enjoyed a rest from driving. When he arrived, a nurse bustled in to inform me that Mr. Crowther was here, and didn't he look the image of Lord Boothby! I suppose there was a faint resemblance to the politician, although Arnold was younger and slimmer than his apparent look-alike.

Arnold brought one of his puppets to keep me company. This was a blonde, lady bellringer, that he had fashioned long before we met. "You see," he said, "I knew I would meet you. I even made a puppet that looks like you."

The days and weeks passed in a languor of sleep, injections and meals, and when he was away, the reading of Arnold's very long letters. Sometimes, two would arrive on the same day. He wrote them anywhere he happened to be - often on trains, and they made exciting reading, because they contained romantic stories of our lives together, in Ancient Egypt. He was quite convinced we had met in a previous life.

Quite suddenly, we were informed that Commonside was closing, and we were going to Lodge Moor Hospital on the outskirts of the city. We left in a fleet of ambulances and I was soon settled in a corner of a spacious, airy ward, for what I hoped would be the final weeks of my convalescence.

After a while, I noticed a new patient in a bed opposite to mine, who whispered to her family when they visited, while nodding in my direction. I knew from her expression that she was not uttering words of approval. I will refer to her as 'Mrs. B'.

I wondered what I had done to deserve the baleful glances she flashed at me. I did not imagine them, because I saw her talking to the Ward Sister, whereupon she, too, glared across at me. The patients that I knew, told me to ignore her, but it was uncomfortable to say the least.

The Ward Sister brought Mrs.B. some angora wool and knitting-needles and I heard that she was going to knit a garment for the Sister. Now, materials such as angora wool, or anything made from animal hair, were banned from the tuberculosis wards for obvious reasons, and I could not believe that the Sister had introduced this substance into the ward.

Mrs. B. would sit knitting away and staring at me from under her specs; until finally I crossed the ward and asked her why I was on the receiving end of her silent hostility. She gave some lame excuse about her glasses, but later, the Sister came up to my bed and said that if I continued to upset Mrs. B. I had better be moved to another bed. I gasped, then said quite plainly that as I had done nothing but lie in my bed, I was certainly not going to move from it. What *was* all this - some kind of persecution? Why not move Mrs. B. if she did not like my face?

For a while, I was left in peace. I could now get dressed and go out for two hours, twice a week. Arnold would drive me away from the hospital - and oh, the relief! My tummy churned when I returned to the ward, and I would dive into bed and close my eyes, for a much longer period than the 'rest time' warranted.

One night, I suddenly awoke to find a pair of glittering black eyes staring down at me, but it was only the Jamaican night nurse who wanted a specimen from me. In hospital, they give you sleeping pills, then wake you up in the middle of the night!

Regular X-rays were taken until they showed that the trouble had cleared up, and a date was set for my discharge. Only the top half of one lung had been affected, but I suppose that was bad enough.

I was feeling much happier until the Sister marched up and said she wanted to see me in her office. It was only a few minutes from the 'rest time', but I imagined it must be something to do with my discharge, and duly trotted along.

When I entered her office, I was treated to a verbal attack in which I was accused of being a trouble-causer, a nuisance, and a bad patient. Once again, I 'saw red', and retaliated in like manner, demanding to know what I had done to deserve this abuse. By way of a reply, the Sister handed me some tablets, saying that they would calm me down. That did it! I threw them on the floor and said she was much more in need of them than I, then with dignity, walked out of the room.

I was very badly shaken, but determined not to break down as I had to walk through the ward, and knew that Mrs. B.'s eyes would miss nothing. I even managed a smile and a word with one or two patients, then I climbed into bed, pulled up the sheets, and cried myself to sleep.

When mother and Arnold heard about it, they decided that the Matron should be informed about the Ward Sister's unprofessional behaviour. Ushered into the Matron's sanctum, I explained what had occurred, and I also mentioned the incident concerning the angora wool! The Matron listened politely, then said she would look into the matter. I think she was as puzzled as we were, but her eyes glinted angrily when the wool was mentioned.

From that moment, there was no further trouble, and the day dawned when I left Lodge Moor Hospital behind. There were patients with whom I had shared a few laughs, and this in spite of the fact that some of them were quite desperately ill. Their courage, in the face of death, was a shining example to all.

The impresario, Pentland Hick had booked us both for a season at the Floral Hall, Scarborough, but now I had these strict instructions to do no further work for at least another three months. So, after a few lazy weeks at home, I joined Arnold in Scarborough. It was so different being able to relax and enjoy an entire summer at my leisure.

The comedian, Leslie Crowther, was also at the Floral Hall that season. We bumped into him at the stage-door, and he remarked, "So, *your* name is 'Crowther', too, is it?" to which Arnold replied in jocular tones, "Yes. Want to make something of it' The comedian looked at us, disdainfully, and walked off.

Actually, Arnold's mother was a Scot, but his father came from Pudsey - and 'Crowther' is a Yorkshire name. After we were married, Arnold teased, "You had to marry me in order to obtain a Yorkshire name." Grandfather William Dawson and his forebears hailed from Dublin, although these 'Sons of David' had a much older Scottish ancestry.

Arnold's father, Cecil Crowther, was an optician who wanted both his sons to follow that profession. Arnold and Norman were fraternal twins coming from separate eggs, so although they shared the same womb, they were disparate in appearance, personality and outlook.

Norman, eventually took over his father's business in Wimbledon, and although Arnold had the same training, he practised stage magic from a very early age, and decided upon a less certain, though much more interesting career in the theatre. When they were born, Mrs. Crowther always hid

Arnold under the blankets of the perambulator, as she considered that giving birth to twin babies at the same time was, "Like an animal" she expected only one child (who if a boy, was to be named, 'Norman'), but when a second baby appeared, she called him after the doctor who delivered them - a Doctor Arnold.

By the age of twenty-eight, Arnold had progressed to producing his own show at the Arcadia Theatre in Scarborough. The year was 1937. Entitled the 'Arnold Crowther Show', one of the acts was a young Beryl Reid, and as she relates in her autobiography, '*So Much Love*' "Arnold Crowther wrote two acts for me, '*The Schoolgirl Impressionist*', and '*My Radio*'."

Reading Beryl s book, it was extraordinary to find that we had played the same theatres, and had also visited out-of-the-way places such as Dunure, in Scotland. We even met the same people in our travels including Arnold Crowther!

Like me, Beryl adored cats, and we also shared the doubtful privilege of having had quite a few bad falls in our time. At the City Varieties Music Hall in Leeds, Beryl caught her heel in the train of her dress and tumbled down a spiral stone staircase. There was no one there to pick her up, so she staggered onto the stage, bottling up her tears until after the show. At birth, Beryl and I shared the qualities of the sign, Gemini. Her sun-sign was Gemini, while I have the Moon, and other astrological aspects in that sign. She thought it was marvellous, that having played so many, and sometimes, outlandish theatres we were still here to tell the tale! Sadly, Beryl Reid has now passed over, but she will be remembered with love and affection by her friends and the public for a very long time.

Midway through that summer in Scarborough, I became very restless and bored, so one night, just for a kick, I joined Arnold on stage, and sang a duet with one of his ventriloquial dolls - a negro called 'Rastus'. He sat on the grand piano I was playing, and we performed a rendition of the 'Banana Boat Song'. It went over well, so I followed it with a solo. My voice had been rested so it was in good form, and the audience wanted more. I needed that 'shot' of applause, it is life-blood to an artiste.

At the beginning of that season, Arnold received a telegram from the B.B.C. Television Centre in London. They wanted him to appear on the 'David Nixon Show' as a guest magician, but Pentland Hick would not release him. I was upset about that, as it could have started an entirely new career for him in television.

The summer of 1958 was spent at the Princess Pavilion in Falmouth, where we stayed with a widow and her dog. She was always talking of her dead husband, and would snarl, "Yes, I said I'd see 'im burn, and I did!" Apparently, her lackless spouse had been cremated. She would grin, evilly, at a small urn on the mantlepiece, muttering, "Yes, you old so-and-so, you old swine - yes!" enjoying her vengeance to the full.

There was no bathroom at her establishment; one had to make do with a tin bath in the kitchen. This, she filled with hot water then left you to it. Not having had the pleasure of such a bath, previously, it was quite an adventure. Her dog was tied up in the kitchen and rarely went out, so we took him for long walks on the beach, which he greatly enjoyed. One day, we found that the landlady had taken up the stair carpet and all the rugs in our bedroom. It appeared that we had been going up and down stairs too much and wearing them out! Almost speechless by this explanation, we said that unfortunately, our feet were our only means of getting from 'a' to 'b', but sarcasm was lost on her.

The parents of the electrician at the theatre, took pity on our plight, and said we could stay with them for the remainder of the season. They were a jolly family who lived in a large, rambling house, and we appreciated returning to the human race once more Of course, most of the places where we stayed during our travels were satisfactory, it is only the bizarre ones that are recalled. At these kind of establishments, Arnold sometimes signed the visitors book with the words, "Quoth the Raven", next to his name, which, always puzzled proprietors. They come from a poem by Walter de la Mare -"Quoth the Raven - never more!"

A story circulated about an artiste, who, feeling under the bed for his slippers, touched something very cold and very different from his footwear. He peered under the bed, and to his horror saw a body lying there! The woman's husband had died and was laid out on the bed, but when her visitor arrived, rather than lose the money, she had put the corpse under it!

I know of one comedian who landed in bad accommodation. Before he left he nailed a kipper behind a cupboard, and an odious smell pervaded the room for several weeks, until the mystified landlady finally discovered its source.

One Christmas season, an agent persuaded us to appear in cabaret on the East Coast, and this proved to be a big mistake. The initial venue was in Immingham, a dreary dockland town with forests of masts and cranes silhouetted against a wintry sky. It was bitter weather, and Arnold had a heavy cold, but he insisted upon fulfilling the contract.

During the evening, Arnold included a spot of pick-pocketing, and inviting a male member of the audience onto the stage to take part in an illusion, he secretly transferred articles from the man's pockets into his own. Then, before his 'assistant' left the stage, Arnold produced the articles, saying, "Oh, don't go without these," giving the mem his comb, pen, or whatever the items were. But, among them there was a small packet, and just in time, Arnold realised what it was and kept it concealed in his pocket. It was a packet of condoms! Afterwards, Arnold always maintained that he was responsible for some female becoming pregnant that Christmas Eve!

We were due in Skegness the following night, so we decided to stay in the area. There was only one hotel in Immingham which looked none too inviting, but Arnold said he felt awful, so we booked in. The bedroom was large and cold with only a tiny electric fire. It had to be constantly fed with coins in order to achieve the minimum of warmth. We spent a miserable night, and next morning, were informed that breakfast could not be served in our room, and in any case, we were too late for it! I managed to obtain tea and toast, and made Arnold stay in bed as long as possible.

Christmas dinner was served late in the afternoon, when the bar had closed. This proved to be uneatable, as everything was either undercooked or burnt. Arnold was worse, and had a temperature, even so, it was a relief to drive off and make our way to Skegness. There, the hotels where we worked, were of a higher standard, warm and cheerful, and bedrooms were put at our disposal for changing purposes. Even trays of food were brought up to us! But I was very relieved when we were at last driving home to Sheffield, having endured the very worst of festive seasons.

What joy it was to be in one's own home, curled up beside a roaring fire. Mother was full of solicitude and bundled Arnold off to bed with a hot toddy or two, and a good, hot meal inside him, but it was some weeks before he fully recovered his health.

On one occasion, Arnold and I gave our services at the Nuffield Centre, a forces canteen near Trafalgar Square. When working in London, most artistes played there and many of them were just making the grade in the sixties -people such as Reg Varney, Benny Hill and Michael Bentine.

I was in my usual dilemma of wondering what numbers to sing, and in the incredibly tiny dressing-room, I continually asked other acts what songs the troops would appreciate the most. I need not have worried, as I went down 'a bomb' as they say. When I came off the stage, someone said, "See! I said you would be O.K.'

While, in the 'Big Smoke', as the capital is called, Arnold showed me some unusual places he had previously discovered. One of them was a small inn at the end of a narrow passage which had been built round a huge tree. Another, was also a hostelry known as "Dirty Dick's". You descended some steps from the road, and entered a bar where all the bottles, ceiling and walls, were covered in dust and cobwebs - hence the name. Tattered old theatre bills and other memorabilia decorated the room, and above the bar hung what looked like a dead weasel. A notice read, "Stroke my fur for luck", and Arnold egged me on, so I did, and the thing leapt at me with a fearful whistling noise, much to the amusement of the other customers. Having now spilt my drink, Arnold grinned at me and ordered another. I must say it was a good ruse for extra sales!

I was introduced, to what for me was a new form of entertaining - that of officiating at various residential hotels over the Christmas period. The Hotel Majestic at St. Anne's-on-Sea; the Queen's Hotel, Chester; the Grand Hotel, Sheringham, and the Grand Hotel, Llandudno, engaged our services during the Christmas holidays for the next six years.

Arnold was familiar with this type of work, but it was a whole new ball-game for me. As Host and Hostess, we provided the cabaret, arranged competitions and games, performed at least one children's show, and generally made ourselves useful.

I was extremely self-conscious at first, as meeting 'the audience' face to face, as it were, was something that did not occur in the theatre. They were out there, beyond the footlights and were thought of a single entity, which from the artistes' point of view, was true.

In these hotels, I was expected to mingle with the guests and discuss trivia with them, which I hated, and the more self-conscious I felt, the more awkward became my position. People began to notice my constraint, as nothing communicates itself more than fear - and it was rapidly coming to that. Happily, I conquered my phobia when I began to regard the entire proceedings as just another 'act'. Then it suddenly became easy! I also realised what shallow lives some people lead, including the well-to-do. One lady sported a magnificent leopard-skin coat which must have cost the earth. She obviously desired to be complimented upon her apparel, as she frequently stroked it during our conversation. So that is what I did, refraining from voicing my true thoughts, namely, that the coat must have looked much better on the leopard!

At the Grand Hotel, Llandudno, a middle-aged couple always celebrated the anniversary of their wedding after midnight on Christmas Eve, and I was requested to accompany the lady on the grand piano, while she sang a selection of songs. However, at 2 a.m. in the morning, and despite the flowing champagne, the specially invited guests were not terribly enthusiastic about her renderings, although she did her best. Apparently, the lady's husband arranged the party so that his wife could have an audience. This may have been true, but there are all kinds of tittle-tattle among so many people.

The food at the Grand Hotel was out-of-this-world, and on Christmas Day, a table, the width of the spacious diningroom, groaned with all manner of succulent provender - even swan! A preserved specimen of the royal bird gazing down, condescendingly, on all the other dishes. (Here, I must stress that today I am a vegetarian. My eyes have been opened to the cruelty most animals suffer in the process of becoming our food and I have no wish to support that process.)

The manager of the hotel was a lovely man, and at the end of our stay he suggested that my mother should come with us the following year. He said, "We cannot have her sitting on her own at such a time, can we?" which was really sweet and thoughtful of him. So in due course, mother accompanied us to Wales. She was ensconced in a super bedroom, had a splendiferous time, and all free of charge!

One of the guests whose name was John, looked the image of the famous actor, Brian Blessed, and I was continually asked if he really was the star. So, with John's permission (who incidentally thoroughly enjoyed the game), we did everything we could to promote this impression, and great fun was had. The Majestic Hotel at St. Anne's-on-Sea, was an enormous pile, and stood in a prominent position on the sea front. Holding some six hundred guests at the festive season, it was chiefly patronised by business people. Here again, there were masses of good things to eat, and at least seven courses for luncheon and dinner, not forgetting tea-time, so that when one meal had been cleared away, it was time for the next to be prepared. Just like the tea-party in "*Alice in Wonderland*". Was this Fate's way of recompensing us for Immingham? Sometimes, there was only an hour and a half between luncheon and tea, but by 4 p.m., everyone was ready to partake of the cream cakes, gateaus, trifles and jellies, the latter items wrought in the most fantastic, decorative designs.

We had to arrange our programmes in good time, so we never stayed too long in the dining-room. We could not afford the waiting time between courses, although we enjoyed all our meals. In any case, I, for one, could not work on a full tummy.

One evening's entertainment was reserved for an incoming cabaret, and of all people, it turned out to be Frank, who had caused me so much distress in the past. I was in the dressing-room at the side of the stage, and when I came out, I nearly fell headlong over some props and cases in the doorway, which had not been there when I entered the room. And, yes, they belonged to Frank, who had very kindly put them there for me to fall over I shouldn't wonder. He was still up to his old tricks!

Arnold suggested a time for his act, but Frank said he would only take orders from the manager of the hotel! However, he returned from the manager's office much subdued, and we learned he had been informed that Mr. Crowther was in charge of the cabaret, and Frank must see *him* about the matter. So that was that. I was relieved when he had gone -he was certainly a trouble causer and had not improved over the years.

Upon our own departure from the Majestic, the manager said we could take any decorations we liked from the rooms and tables. These were really lovely, so we left with armfuls of pretty baubles which we incorporated in our own celebrations at home.

Although the pattern of my life changed after meeting Arnold, the work went on and on. I suppose I was lucky to be always thus engaged, but there were times when I longed to be out of the public eye for a while.

A summer season in North Wales proved to be hard work but had its frivolous side, too. The company at the New Coliseum Theatre in Rhyl included my old friend, Charlie Ellis, but sadly he became ill and had to return home to London where he passed away. His place was filled by Roy Rolland, a comedian who also featured impersonations of "Old Mother Riley". Roy had been a stand-in and understudy for Arthur Lucan in his films as the famous Irish beldame - not forgetting, "her daughter, Kitty" (Arthur's wife, Kitty MacShane). Roy was a great character who was always good for a laugh.

Most summer shows included an "Old Tyme Music Hall" programme, and I had developed an impersonation of Ella Shields singing her famous song, "Burlington Bertie from Bow", complete with ragged frock-coat, top hat, and cane. This number proved to be a hit, so much so that during the season at Rhyl, I began to receive fan-mail, albeit of the oddest kind! It appeared that most of the writers were Lesbian ladies, as many of the letters went way beyond the complimentary stages, and described, in explicit terminology, what they desired of me! Arnold roared with laughter and said he had not realised that Rhyl was a hotbed of homosexuals. Come to that, neither had I!

20. As 'Burlington Bertie From Bow' in 'Old Tyme Music Hall'

Apropos the above, the term 'lesbian' is a misnomer when used in reference to female homosexuals. It was coined from the name, Lesbos, a small Greek island where once lived Sappho, the greatest poetess the world has known. Strabo's comment of Sappho is apt: 'a miracle of a young woman". She ran an academy for young ladies and taught them speech development, deportment, dancing, and most of the social graces. That some of her poetry reveals a marvellous appreciation and intoxication for feminine beauty is undeniable, and yet we know that she married and bore a daughter - Cleis. Therefore, Sappho cannot truly be classed as a homosexual, though whether she was a sexual invert or not, is a question that can never be answered.

A more decorous note came from a woman who invited me to meet her on a specific date, after the show. She would be waiting in her car to take me out for a meal; an invitation that I courteously declined. Nevertheless, the letters proved the authenticity of my impersonation and also gave an added piquancy to the 'Music Hall' evenings.

Before the season ended we had been 'seen' and booked for the following summer, at the Derbyshire Miners Holiday Camp, also situated in Rhyl.

When that season's show commenced everything went well until we rehearsed for an 'Old Tyme Music Hall' programme. The manager, who was also the comedian in the show, one Sonnie Roy, took me aside and said, "We don't want you to do the 'Ella Shields' number, Pat, we want you to sing a song in period dress." This remark completely floored me, after all he had seen my work the previous year and had booked me on the strength of it. He also knew how well the 'male' number went over, and there was no one else performing a similar one. What was going on? I smiled to myself, suddenly remembering those letters. Had they heard about them? Then, Bill, the husband of Dianne (a double act), who had also seen the show at the Coliseum, but had no jurisdiction over me, ambled up and said the same thing. And although I repeatedly requested an explanation for their absurd restriction, none was forthcoming.

I talked the matter over with Arnold, but he was as mystified us myself, and then I started to think rationally about the problem.

Why should they be so opposed to this tried and tested number, completely in accord with the 'Old Tyme Music Hall' tradition? Could it be that another artiste wanted to shine and was afraid that I would take some of their glory? Now, Dianne, a very buxom lady, was impersonating Sophie Tucker. Could this be the reason? Very soon, a little bird told me that it was!

I had heard of this kind of thing occurring in show business, and recalled how a contract promised me for a big revue, failed to materialise. The leading lady - Frances Day, stipulated that she must be the only blonde in the show. This was explained to me, with apologies, by the impresario concerned.

I was angry, not least because a good number had been wasted through petty jealousy. How dare they do such a despicable thing at the expense of the show? I had to swallow my pride, but my feathers were decidedly ruffled and I was determined to overcome such unfair treatment.

As the Edwardian artiste, Ellaline Terriss, I chose to sing, "When you were sweet sixteen", in a black velvet, off the shoulder gown, with a bustle effect. My blood was up and I was going to do my best despite everything. I sang a few bars off-stage, then walked on, finishing to resounding applause. I thought, "Follow that!" Subsequent summers were spent at Warner Brothers Holiday Centres; four of them at Puckpool, near Ryde, on the Isle of Wight.

One particular week during the season was more hectic than all the others. This was Carnival Week, which included a procession through Ryde and a Fancy Dress competition by the entertainers and members of the staff. For Arnold and myself, all this was in addition to the usual programmes of the week which included a revue, a cabaret, 'Old Tyme Music Hall' (which featured the 'Ella Shields' impression!); three children's shows a day; the children's own show (produced by 'yours truly' plus daily rehearsals), and a sing-song on Saturday evening when we were introduced to a new batch of holiday-makers.

In our first season at Warners, "France throughout the Ages" (an idea of Arnold's), was chosen for the Carnival procession. All the holiday centres on the island took part, and Puckpool entered a number of floats. As 'Joan of Arc', I was tied to a stake on the top of a lorry; another, featured 'Napoleon' and 'Josephine' reclining on a bed, and one float represented the cathedral of Notre Dame, with a huge bell which tolled continuously by way of an amplified recording - it looked very impressive and was expertly constructed by the carpenters who worked at Puckpool. Gus, a resident entertainer, took the part of the Hunchback, with a dark-haired beauty, as the gypsy girl, Esmeralda. Gus, like Arnold, was ace at make-up and made an excellent Quasimodo. One float depicted the French Revolution with a realistic guillotine and notices which read, "Ask for short back and sides!" and "Necks please!"

As 'Joan', dressed in a cotton shift and wearing an auburn wig, it was a painful three hours for me. The ropes which bound me to the stake, cut into my body so that the journey through the town of Ryde was agony. Every time the vehicle stopped, pain surged through me where the ropes restricted movement. Still, what little pain to that endured by The Maid herself! Arnold, dressed as a priest, held up a cross in front of me, and two other men wearing black masks, were the executioners. Joan's personal escutcheon, the 'Crowned Sword', decorated the sides of the vehicle.

21. As 'Joan of Arc', in the carnival procession at Ryde, Isle of Wight.

The streets were lined with people, and when our float passed by there were cries of "Anyone got a match?", to which a voice replied, "Yes! My arse and your face!" Amid the general good humour of the crowds, a man shouted, "Can I have chips with that?" Incidentally, Ryde was one of the places Gerald Gardner took Donna on their honeymoon, and where he taught her to shoot with a pistol.

For the Fancy Dress Competition that season, I chose the character of 'Queen Nerfertiti' with a little boy walking behind me. His skin was stained brown and he carried a large fan on a pole. Arnold made the unique headdress of this Egyptian queen out of papier mache, and I embroidered the skirt with shiny, coloured raffia and covered the orange cape with blue anksatas (the Ancient Egyptian symbol of life). I tanned my skin for effect and carried the Crook and the Flail. We knew that this queen would be unfamiliar to most of the campers, but even so there was great difficulty in establishing who had won first prize - 'Queen Nerfertiti' or 'Dracula's Daughter'. The audience were requested to applaud each of us in turn, and this went on for at least fifteen minutes with the judges still unable to decide. Finally, they awarded first prize to my 'rival' and I took the second prize. The Entertainments Manager later confided that he had given the travelling clock (first prize) to me, anyway. Such duplicity!

In the men's section, Arnold went as 'The Mummy', and I had to wrap him up in strips of linen, smeared with glue. When his head had been bandaged, he wanted a drink, so he had to sip it through a straw.

Previously, one of the kitchen staff asked Arnold what he should go as, and seeing that the chap was short and thin, Arnold said, "Go as 'Groucho Marx', you only need a cigar and a moustache for that." His advice was taken, and the man won first prize!

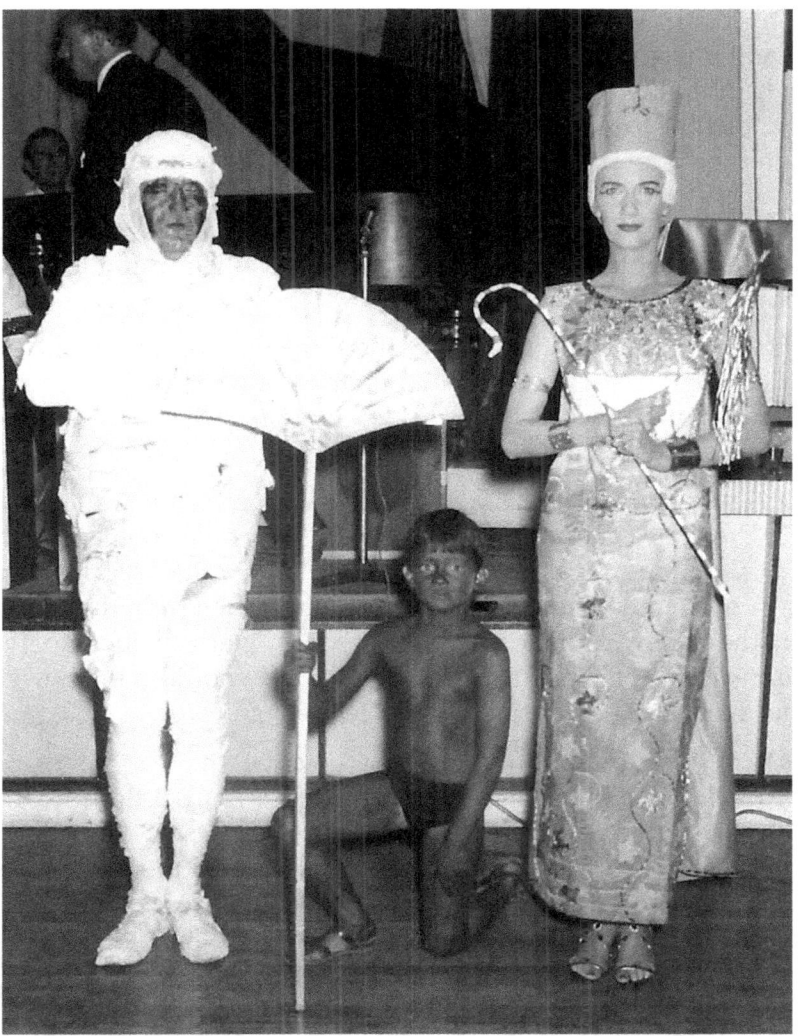

22. Arnold as 'The Mummy', self as 'Queen Nerfertiti', and obliging young holiday-maker as my attendant; his dark skin was obtained from a bottle!

During the seasons we worked for Warners, Arnold entered this event in many wonderful guises, such as 'The Devil Rides Out', 'The Man in the Iron Mask', and 'The Werewolf'. I soon caught on to the popularity of monsters, so on two occasions my offering was 'The Bride of Frankenstein', and no one knew who was under the make-up! When a hand was held over my head for the applause, the ballroom erupted in wild cheers. I was an easy winner, and on the 'lap of honour' walked round to more cries of approbation.

It was at Puckpool that I met the film star, Oliver Reed. As a friend of Gus, he dropped into the bar one evening, accompanied by two pretty girls - one on either side - so that they appeared to be permanent appendages!

To relate everything of interest that happened while we worked for the Warner Brothers would take a book on its own. But one incident that struck everyone who worked for them as amusing, was when the three Warner Brothers descended from the clouds in their private helicopter. Their visits were likened to the appearance of the Holy Trinity, when we should have bowed our heads to the ground in suitable homage.

My favourite season would have to be the one spent on Anglesey, although Sheringham, in Norfolk, runs a close second and for quite disparate reasons. It was in Sheringham that I discovered the Tarot cards. An antique shop in the main street was always stuffed with goodies at reasonable prices, and I was often poking around in there.

One day, Arnold came along too, and pointed to something on one of the shelves. It was a small leather box, and upon examination, was found to contain a pack of Tarot cards, together with a tiny begrimed pamphlet of instructions that was practically falling apart. They had obviously been used for many years, and I wondered to whom they had belonged.

23. Lighting a cigarette for Arnold's 'Andy'.

Although there are very many different sets of the Tarot, I never came across that particular deck, again. The children on the 'Sun' card were dressed in the 30's style, which gave a clue to their age, and the box was hand-made from pieces of stout leather, bound together with soft twine. They were purchased for a modest amount and became the means whereby I committed the cards to memory and eventually became a Tarot consultant.

That same day, we discovered another treasure. Leaning against the leg of a table was a large book cover made from two pieces of polished wood, hinged with leather. The front was incised with the letter 'A' standing proud and surrounded by carved oak leaves, acorns, vine leaves and grapes. It cost only five shillings.

Without realising it at the time, these two items were signposts to the future. They were 'gifts' which indicated and coincided with the spiritual journey upon which I was about to embark. By studying the Tarot I became familiar with occult symbolism; the Major Arcana explaining the soul's evolution towards Godhead. And through actually reading them, I was given information on how to proceed from that particular point in my life. The beautiful cover eventually became the receptacle for my *Book of Shadows*, and now reposes upon a lectern (made by Arnold), in my temple. For those readers who are unfamiliar with the Craft of the Wise, or Book of Shadows, or B.O.S., is a hand-written volume of rituals, prayers, and secrets of working magic, which is handed down from one witch to another.

We wondered if both these items had belonged to the same person. If so, had that person been a witch? The significant initial on the book-cover, combined with the carvings of oak and vine was enough to stir the imagination. The letter 'A' being the most prolific initial in the names of the Goddess, both in Britain and elsewhere in the world. Often, if there is no one with whom to leave their magical writings, a witch will burn the book, rather than allow it to fall into unknown bands. Had the book-cover once protected another B.O.S.? Stranger things have happened.

24. The "Bride of Frankenstein's Monster" at Warner Bros. Holiday Centre, Puckpool, Isle Of Wight.

25. Entertaining at a children's hospital in Edinburgh. Photo: Ian Lilleyman

In 1991 and 1998, I returned to Sheringham on holiday, and the antique shop was still there! Although not so well-stocked with curios as before, on both occasions I managed to obtain some interesting items. A horse brass with a pentagram engraved upon it (a symbol of the Craft), a handsome brass ram's head, and an old plaque of the Sun God. I also bought a number of gifts for friends who I knew appreciated unusual and rare objects.

At the time of my first visit to Sheringham, all those years before, the wheel of my life was about to turn once more. I had come to the years of discovery - of the reasons for this incarnation, beyond the mundane. In astrological terminology I had reached the Saturn Return. This occurs when the planet Saturn returns to the place it occupied at the time of birth; a period of around 29 years. It is said that this aspect always brings major changes into the life - in line with the personal birth-chart, the character, and whatever else the chart reveals. The aspect begins when Saturn comes within orb of its original position, when a person is about 27 years old, and ends at the age of say, 34. So, sometime during these years, and usually in a particular period, the effect will occur. It certainly did for me!

Chapter 5
A Magical World

Arnold and I finally found the time to visit Gerald Gardner on the Isle of Man. He lived at Castletown in a gem of an old farmhouse situated in Malew Street. A small door in the bathroom connected the house to a barn comprising of two stories. The top floor of the barn held Gerald's Magic Circle as well as hundreds of books which lined the rough stone walls. An ancient carved sideboard fashioned with many cupboards and secret drawers occupied a position between the small door and one of the windows, while old swords and pieces of armour decorated any available space on the walls. Beautifully wrought incense burners and lamps from distant lands hung from the great beams, and the aroma of incense permeated everything in this unique chamber.

Gerald Gardner's Museum of Witchcraft and Magic lay only a few minutes walk from his house and was part of the buildings which surrounded the Witches Mill, once the meeting-place of the famous Arbory witches. It was an ideal position for the museum and also contained a restaurant and a ballroom.

When I met Gerald face to face, I was immediately drawn to him. Here was an individual of great intelligence and charm; someone who had travelled widely over the years and accumulated an immense amount of knowledge in many diverse subjects. I soon learned that he also had a very dry sense of humour and regarded the everyday world with a detached yet tolerant air of resignation. He was 76 years young when we met in 1960, a tall, wiry man who refused to allow the advancing years to dominate his activities.

26. Self and Doreen Valiente

Gerald's local mode of transport was a bicycle which he used every day, mostly between his home and the museum. He could be seen free-wheeling down a steep street, his white hair streaming behind him in the wind. He was certainly an archetype of his sun-sign - Gemini. Gerald's life is still being documented in various books and television programmes, because as well as having had such an interesting existence he was the person responsible for the renaissance of the Old Religion in the 1950's. His own initiation into the Mysteries of the Goddess took place in 1939 at the home of Dorothy St. Quintin Fordham who lived at the Mill House near the village of Highcliffe, in the New Forest. His investigations into the ancient beliefs and magical practices of various cultures in the world had finally culminated in his homeland, most of his life having been spent in the Far East where he became a customs official for the British Government, retiring in 1936.

Upon his return to England, where he was to change the face of British history, he continued to explore such things as spiritualism and magic, and occasionally worked for the British Museum where his expertise on the Kris - the magical curved dagger of the natives in Malaya, was often required. Gerald's authorship of *Kris and Other Malay Weapons*, published at Singapore in 1936, had resulted in his being considered the world authority on these sacred knives, and may also have earned him the honorary distinction of Doctor of Philosophy, though this has never been proved. However, in her book, *The Rebirth of Witchcraft*, Doreen Valiente says that in the Far East it was customary for almost any learned person to be given the courtesy title of 'Doctor'.

On a sea voyage in 1938, Gerald started to write a novel entitled, *A Goddess Arrives*. Written over a year before his initiation took place, the book reveals that his knowledge of the ancient matriarchal religion was already established at the time.

27. Gerald Brosseau Gardner

The story of my own initiation by Gerald Gardner, into the Craft of the Wise, and my eventual ordination to the position of High Priestess of the Goddess, has been told elsewhere, suffice to say that my life, and the way in which I viewed the world, had changed forever. Each soul must seek its own way towards enlightenment. For me, that way was the Path of the Goddess and Her Mysteries. This is not the common or garden type of witchcraft, however worthy that may be, but the ancient Priesthood of the Old Religion which became known as the coven of 13. It is interesting to note that although in most people's minds, the term 'witch' immediately conjures up some evil person dealing out dark, nefarious deeds, the Germanic root of the word 'witch' gives it as meaning, 'something which is sacred', or 'that which is made sacred'.

The roots of witchcraft (or what became known as witchcraft), have descended from Ancient Egypt, Babylon, Suma and Albion, the latter being the original name for Britain and meaning, 'The White Island'. Witchcraft has nothing to do with the popular media misconception of Devil worship, or anything dreamed up by newspaper reporters. But, because the rites and rituals are usually performed without clothes, or 'sky-clad' as adherents would say, and because most people have been brought up to regard the human body as 'not very nice', or words to that effect, it is immediately assumed that the witches are up to all kinds of naughtiness. Nothing could be further from the truth! Witches believe that they are made in the image of the gods, therefore, there is nothing in the least abhorrent about the human body.

The reasons behind initiation into the Craft are very serious ones and echo the aspirations of most schools of the Mysteries. In the main, they concern taking an oath before the Altar of the Goddess - "to keep most secret all that you have passed through in the Circle"; learning the ways of working magic;

considerations on the evolution of the soul; the use of the magical imagination; training the mind through prayer and meditation, and the working out of negative Karma from previous lives which initiation usually evokes.

28. Gerald Gardner's house in Malew Street, Castletown, Isle of Man as it looks today. Photo: Ian Lilleyman

I was very lucky to have Arnold as my magical partner in the Craft. I had initiated him with Gerald's guidance and instructions, after my own initiation. This is the way in which the Craft is handed down, from man to woman, and from woman to man. And a few months later, (on the 9th November, 1960, to be exact), Arnold and I were married at the Registry Office in Sheffield. Our wedding received worldwide publicity in the press, with local placards proclaiming. "The Witches Wed"

My husband was no stranger to psychic experiences. One of them concerned a previous incarnation of his. It occurred during World War II when he joined E.N.S.A., entertaining the troops in the various theatres of war. He was stationed in Paris for a period, and a fellow officer introduced Arnold to a clairvoyant, Madam Brux. She spoke English fluently, and proceeded to read the palms of both men. She gave Arnold a reading which could apply to most people, then suddenly stared at him and exclaimed, "Do you feel you have had other lives?" Arnold said, he didn't know, then, "I believe you have, and that you were once a Buddhist Monk. What do you think?" Arnold replied, "That's interesting. After all I am a Libran and keep to the Middle Path, and I belonged to the Buddhist Society in London, before the war. I even own a carved wooden Buddha that was given to me when I was very young," Madam Brux was excited. She persuaded Arnold and his companion to attend a seance a friend of hers was holding in the near future. This person was a well-known medium in Paris, and Arnold thought it was too good an opportunity to miss.

The medium was a very old lady who spoke only French, but Madam Brux said she would translate any messages that came through for their English visitors. Along with other guests, they were requested to spread their hands on the table, with their little fingers, touching. The people smiled and nodded to the newcomers, and when they had settled down, the medium went into a trance and was soon giving messages which were duly acknowledged by one or other of the guests. Then the medium spoke again. "It's for you," whispered Madam Brux, "I'll translate it for you." She listened, attentively, "A man is coming through who says he was once your teacher. Now, he is your guide. You were a student in a Lamasary in Tibet. I'm afraid, you were killed. There is a name - Younghusband."

29. Standing beside Gerald's Museum of Witchcraft at Castletown, Isle of Man. The restaurant, ballroom and the top of the witches mill are also in view. This picture was taken long after the museum had been sold. Photo: Ian Lilleyman

When the seance was over, Arnold wrote down the entire message, but a totally unexpected thing occurred just after the message was given. There was a loud bang on the table, which made some of the sitters jump up from their chairs. The light was switched on, and there, lying on the table, was a prayer-wheel! "Wonderful!" cried Madam Brux, "it's an apport!" Arnold had to laugh, "You mean to say that this object flew through the air from goodness knows where, to end up on this table?" Madam, bridled, visibly, "Yes, I do!" Arnold grinned at his friend and shook his head, "I don't know what you take me for, but I happen to be a stage magician, so I know all the tricks." Then he suddenly realised how rude he was being. If they thought it was necessary to perform parlour tricks, so be it, after all the two of them had been invited to the seance. Arnold apologised for his rudeness, but Madam waved the matter aside. "Do not worry. Here, take the prayer-wheel, it was yours in a previous life. You will receive the other artefacts that were once yours in due course - from other sources."

The medium, awakened from her trance by the noise, was being comforted by some of her friends, so when Arnold and his companion had offered their profuse thanks for the demonstration, they departed into the night air of the Paris streets.

Patricia Crowther - From Stagecraft to Witchcraft

30. Replacing a candlestick after a meeting at
Gerald Gardner's covenstead in Castletown, Isle of Man.

Arnold asked his friend if he had received any information, but apparently there had been no message for him, although, when his palm was read, Madam Brux had said that he would not return to England, but would probably stay in France. "I've always loved the place," he said, "I may settle here after the war." Arnold was moved from France soon afterwards but one day he was informed that his friend had been killed in an air-raid and he recalled the words of Madam Brux, that he would remain in France. She must have seen his death!

Strange as it may be, after the war, an acquaintance of Arnold's presented him with a small, brass cup that he had picked up on an antique stall. He thought Arnold could find some use for it in his act. Arnold, however, took it to the British Museum and was told that it was a butter-lamp from Tibet. Originally, it would have been filled with butter, and a wick inserted into it. There was no doubt that it was a ceremonial object from a Tibetan shrine to the Buddha.

A musician friend asked Arnold if he would look for a tom-tom drum when he was on torn. My husband found one in a curio shop in Dundee, so he purchased it for his friend. The man in the shop said it was Indian, but while Arnold was examining it in his hotel, another guest said he was almost sure that the drum was Tibetan and one used in religious rites. He also commented that there was another, similar type of drum which was composed of human skulls. So Arnold quite naturally decided to keep the drum, and look for another one for the musician.

Back in London, he began hunting round the antique shops, and after a considerable time, he discovered a skull-drum in a district called Seven Dials. The owner of the shop wanted a great deal of money for it, saying it was an exceedingly rare curio, but Arnold haggled with him and obtained it at a more reasonable price, although he still thought he had paid too much.

A few weeks later, he discovered a Tibetan trumpet fabricated from a human thigh-bone. Surely, this was more than coincidence? He decided to consult an expert at the British Museum; obtained an appointment and took along his collection.

He was informed that the articles were genuine and peculiar to a certain type of monk. This was the Z'i-jed-pa (The Mild Doer), a homeless mendicant of the Yogi class who belonged to no particular sect, but had an affinity with the Kar-gyu-pa. The expert said that these monks were now practically extinct but were nevertheless regarded as saints who would experience Nirvana when they died. Their appurtenances consisted of thigh-bone trumpets, skull-drums, and the usual butter lamps and prayer-wheels. A particularly unsavoury requirement of them was the eating of a morsel of skin from the human corpse when preparing the trumpet and the drum.

The order was founded by P'a-dam-pa Sans-rgyas (Juanaka OR Pita-Buddha) from Jara Sin(d)ha, in India. This man journeyed through Kashmir and Na-ri to Tibet in the twelfth century A.D.

Arnold even came across a postcard showing exactly this type of beggar-monk, and carrying the above-mentioned items upon his person. The discovery of such a rare picture seemed to substantiate the information he had already received, as though Fate was saying, "Well, you have been given all the implements, now here is the monk, himself!"

So, according to the 'evidence', Arnold had been a beggar-monk in a previous life, probably his last one. But he had certainly not attained Nirvana, as he had been born again. What had gone wrong? He began attending meetings of the Buddhist Society at the Caxton Hall, and talked to people, there. They said it was quite possible for Arnold to have been a monk, previously, but that he must have done something very wrong to incur yet another life upon Earth. It would have had to be a serious act of wrong-doing, and even if the crime was one of self-defence, it would still not justify the act. If he had lifted his hand to harm another living soul, he would no longer have been considered to be a Buddhist and would have to expiate this negative Karma in another lifetime. Sobered by this conversation, Arnold left the building, never to return.

31. Doreen Valiente and self toasting the Old Ones.

The following year, he attended an exhibition of Tibetan artefacts and curios, held in Bond Street, and discovered the missing link in the mystery. Upon entering the hall, the first thing he saw was a name which took him back to the Paris clairvoyant, all those years ago. The exhibition classified the collection of a man who had headed a military attack against Tibet in 1904 - his name was Colonel Younghusband! Could this have been when he killed someone? Filled with a desire to confirm these speculations, Arnold went to see a medium who was considered to be proficient in her art.

After listening to his story, the medium went into a meditative trance, then gave him the following information. She thought he had indeed been a Tibetan monk of some kind, and saw him lying on the ground, bleeding from a wound in the chest. She felt that he had been attacked by a soldier, whom he had managed to repulse, but in the ensuing skirmish, the soldier had accidentally fallen over a high parapet. Arnold, himself, was slain by another soldier, a few minutes afterwards.

The strange thing about this last account, is that of time. If Arnold had been killed in 1904 in that military attack against Tibet, he was reborn very quickly into a life as 'Arnold Crowther' in 1909. I say, 'very quickly', because from what I have learned, unless the soul has gained wisdom through various lives on Earth, the usual 'time' between incarnations can represent a hundred years or more, although time, as we know it, does not exist on the spiritual Planes. And if the medium's vision was an accurate one, a fatal similarity occurred between Arnold's death as a monk, from a wound in the chest, and his eventual passing in this life, from an illness which originated in the same area of his body, namely, his chest!

It is said that for souls who have experienced many lifetimes, the descent into matter becomes more and more transient and unimportant. Soon after his death, the soul of the Dalai Lama is looked for in a new-born child. The monks are given certain signs and omens concerning the baby's whereabouts, and astrologers and mediums are requested to find the Dalai Lama in his new body. It is amazing how the child, once discovered, finds his own possessions and toys, from a pile of disparate items, and is neither solemn nor humourless in his disposition. He readily takes to the duties laid upon him with a serenity and grace which reveal his soul's sagaciousness.

Arnold was born (or reborn) in the centre of the sign of Libra - the 6th October, said to be the unluckiest day of the year on which to be born although I have never discovered why this should be so. He walked the Middle Path and would never take sides in an argument or discussion even when he knew who was in the right, which could be infuriating at times. He was able to detach himself from surrounding influences, good or bad, and said he would be happy living with me in a mud hut! Arnold observed the world without being greatly affected by it, but he always insisted that we had met in a previous life.

Apropos of the above, Arnold's rebirth could have been achieved through taking the body of the second fraternal twin. Because it is said that if it so wills, an 'old soul' can obtain rebirth in a particular and chosen time-frame and place, through this method. Apparently, not possible if the twins are identical, coming from a single egg which divides into two identical babies.

I was now ordained as a High Priestess of the Goddess and thus entitled to form my own coven, if I so wished. I was very keen on the idea, but realised the difficulties involved. Genuine covens - those which evolve round a person who has received initiation from a consecrated High Priest or High Priestess, down the line, are very different from covens built by a self-initiated witch, whose only knowledge stems from reading books on the subject. There are hundreds of the latter type of coven, today; 'witches' who believe in 'doing their own thing' as it were, but I was taught that there is only one way to enter the Craft - to become a 'Child of the Goddess' - and that is to be initiated by someone like Gerald Gardner, whose pedigree as a

High Priest and Elder, fulfilled all the conditions, including one of the most important - that of passing on the power!

Being the recipient of magical knowledge handed down through the generations, cannot be regarded lightly. It can prove to be both a blessing and a curse. A blessing, because you have been considered worthy to receive the secrets so closely guarded by the ancestors. A curse, knowing that you must never err in your judgement if you wish to pass the secrets to another witch. Your life, thereafter, must be lived according to the ethics of the Craft, and the trust that was placed in you by your initiator.

The inception of the Sheffield Coven took place in December 1961 when the first member was initiated. It has now been in operation for 40 years and has seen many adherents progress through the degrees of advancement, then leave, with our blessings, to form covens of their own. When this occurs, it is always a special delight to me. It makes all the work so very worthwhile. Another great joy is working magic for people who write to us. These are usually requests for a return to good health, during a prolonged illness. And when the coven has decided upon a particular case, we ask for a photograph and a lock of hair to obtain a link with the person. The coven only deals with one request during a meeting; concentrating, for at least half- an-hour, upon the part of the person to be healed. There have been many positive results from our work, sometimes when the medical profession has given no hope of a cure. We do not devalue the work of doctors in any way, but there is a time when higher aid is needed - at least according to the letters we receive! I know from experience that Magic does work, and I believe that in the future, mind power and medicine will join forces. What a puissant *force* that would be!

During the last twenty years, the Sheffield coven has concentrated upon aiding the many charities which work against cruelty to animals - in all its many forms. And although this is an on-going project which never seems to end, there have been quite amazing successes; workings which I have put a tick against, as every meeting of the coven is documented.

On a lighter note, I have met occultists of various persuasions, many of whom have been interesting characters in one way or another. I was regressed by a hypnotist on several occasions, and brought forth some intriguing, discarnate personalities from the distant past. The hypnotist would put me into a light trance, then by suggestion, take me back to an earlier century. He would then ask who I was, or, if anyone was there.

Often, there was no reply, but one night a young girl came through who said her name was Phillipa Towyn and that she had lived in Gosport. She said that she went to church three times on Sundays; owned a black pony called Satan, and that she, and her brother, Richard, often went sailing in their small boat- Her mother was always ill in bed, so Phillipa had all the housework to do, and as a result was often very tired. When questioned as to the name of the church she attended, Phillipa said it was called, St John's. Years later, we met someone from Gosport who confirmed that there had indeed been a St. John's church there, but it was destroyed by a bomb in the last war.

Now, when Phillipa came through, the hypnotist had taken me back to the year 1539, then later, he suggested the year 1590, and again, Phillipa spoke and said she was sixty-five years old (this would have made her around fourteen years of age, the first time). Apparently, she had never married, as her lover had been killed in the wars. She mentioned Drake, Raleigh and Essex, and said that Leicester was in the Tower of London. Asked who was on the British throne, she replied, 'Good Queen Bess'. This was interesting, in that Phillipa did not say, 'Queen Elizabeth' but described the Queen in the way most of her subjects would have done with the more affectionate, 'Good Queen Bess'.

An old woman came through regularly. Her name was Polly, and she had been a witch, so ever after, we called her, "Polly, the

Witch". When asked about spells, she would pronounce them very quickly in rhyme without faltering, and the very fact that they *were* in rhyme, and many of considerable length, made the communications all the more genuine. Arnold wrote everything down, but he found it very difficult to capture these spells on paper, due to the speed in which they were spoken.

Polly said she had lived in the seventeenth century, in a small cottage with a collection of various animals. She was scathing in her opinion of the people who sought her services. Her old, cracked voice filled the room and I was told that her presence was very strong. I think that even the hypnotist was astonished at the phenomena he had conjured up! As for me, I did nothing except lend Polly my vocal chords, and tried to listen, with my inner ear (without much success), to what she was saying. It was a very strange feeling. The spells she gave were very down-to-earth ones, and it was obvious that Polly had been the local wise-woman of the district, as opposed to belonging to the Priesthood of the Craft, although she may have been a member of a coven at some time in her life.

One of these spells was to make a man return to his wife. Polly said she was often asked for this one! It consisted of mixing the moon-blood of the wife with either hairs from the errant husband's head, or scraps of apparel which carried his sweat. These items were mixed together in a pan, with a little water, over a hot fire, concentrating on what was desired, and chanting the following incantation: -

"Get thee a man. Get thee a maid,
Mix it up well, be not afraid,
This you will get, this he will eat,
Mix it with bread. Mix it with meat."

If the husband was no longer living in the matrimonial home, Polly gave another chant for this spell: -

> *"Blood of a bat, hair of a cat,*
> *Skin of the man, mix if you can,*
> *Hair of a goat, blood of a stoat.*
> *This you will mix, until him you fix"*

The woman then sewed these ingredients into a little red bag and wore it secretly, next to her skin. The 'skin of the man' might be obtained from flakes of dead skin adhering to the husband's stockings. Polly said she knew hundreds of spells and they all worked! She volunteered one to make the crops grow strong and tall. This was usually performed by villagers, with a witch to lead them, dancing in a circle round a field, astride a broom or a pole. The chant Polly gave, was as follows: -

> *"Leap in the air. Do it with prayer.*
> *The crops will grow high;*
> *Up to the sky.*
> *As high as you jump,*
> *So high will they grow.*
> *Greet thee the Sun,*
> *Greet thee the Moon,*
> *High will we jump,*
> *Much higher a-soon.*
> *Our crops will grow high,*
> *Up to the sky!"*

The above verse is an excellent example of sympathetic magic - the most ancient form of magic in the world. It was a prayer, combined with suitable actions to show what was required, so that with the aid of the Gods, Nature would copy these actions, and the crops would grow as high as the dancers leapt in the air. In those days, people believed in the Ancient Providence the original source of all things - the spiritual power behind the Universe - changeless and eternal. Witches and neo-pagans still recognise these unseen energies which radiate from living matter, permeate everything and originate from realms other than the physical plane. They have learned that the life-force comes from the Unmanifest and brings everything into being. They understand that our world is the *effect* of the Unmanifest that it informs and enlivens matter and is the active cause behind manifestation.

Occultists used to call it 'the Great Magical Agent' and regarded it as the necessary ingredient in magical operations. Today, witches see it as a 'border-line energy' which is all pervading. It is undoubtedly the *modus operandi* of magic, which is often termed, 'the art of getting results'.

Doreen Valiente, whom I met in the sixties, was a very good friend of mine. She was also a High Priestess of the Craft having been initiated by Gerald Gardner in 1953. Doreen lived in Brighton, and Arnold and I often visited her during summer shows on the south coast of England, and sometimes spent a holiday in Brighton after the close of a season. On one occasion, Doreen visited us in Sheffield, and attended our Hallowe'en meeting - the only time we had fourteen witches in the Circle! It was while we were staying in Brighton, however, that we paid a visit to the 'Long Man of Wilmington', a chalk-cut hill figure on the Sussex Downs. A few days later, Andrew Demain (a London witch), called to see Doreen, and when we mentioned the 'Long Man' he wanted to see it, too. So, it was decided to conduct a nocturnal ritual in the natural hollow which lies at the top of the hill, above the figure. Andrew would not actually see the figure, as it must be viewed from the valley and preferably in day-light, but he thought a meeting there, would be much more worthwhile. The weather forecast was not good, but we decided to defy the elements.

Leaving the car safely parked, we climbed the steep sides of the tor in the last vestiges of daylight and had not gone far when it started to rain By the time we had gained the summit it was coming down in stair-rods, but we persevered and performed the rite. Our candles were safely inside lanterns, and above us, the grey clouds, illumined by our small flames, enveloped us in a dark canopy. It seemed as if we were inside those clouds. The candlelight projected and magnified our shadows onto them; it was as though we were in the company of the Gods, themselves!

The rite completed, we packed everything away and set off down the hill. It was pitch-black and the rain had churned the ground into a squelchy morass of clay, which made the steep slope difficult to negotiate. My own torch was of little use in that kind of weather, but I realised it was not the route by which we had ascended the hill. Doreen was some way ahead when I suddenly shouted, "Stop!", for no reason I could think of at the time. She obeyed my instruction, and when I caught up with her, the light from my torch showed where the ground disappeared, a few steps further on. We had certainly lost the track because my friend had nearly walked off the edge of a quarry!

We were all visibly shaken, not least Doreen, herself "What made you call out to me?" she asked "How did you know?" I said it must have been my sixth sense, and I recalled a foggy night in Birmingham when my landlady's husband walked me home, and a similar incident occurred. Doreen said, "It's funny, but when you shouted 'Stop!', I seemed to feel a hand on my shoulder, but you were some way behind me." I said that the Gods must also have helped in saving her life, and everyone agreed.

We struck off in another direction, where the welcoming sight of car headlights strobed the darkness of the valley. Soon, we were heading for Brighton, and despite protective clothing, quite soaked to the skin.

Back at Doreen's flat, we peeled off our sodden clothes and wrapped ourselves in warm blankets, Cassie, (Doreen's husband), plied us with mugs of hot tea and plates of toasted muffins, but rather tactlessly commented upon how wet we all were, whereupon Doreen replied, acidly, "Well, Dear one does tend to get wet when it rains."

In the early hours of the morning, we returned to our hotel and fell into bed, but an hour or so later, the breakfast bell shot us awake. I grabbed a piece of paper and immediately scribbled down a verse which came into my head as I woke.

I called this poem "*Awakening*", and it appeared in my book *Lid Off the Cauldron* (published by Capall Bann?.

The rite on the top of the 'Long Man' was one of the most difficult I have ever encountered, but the poem revealed that through pilgrimages to ancient, sacred sites (not necessarily undertaken in such arduous conditions), something of worth can often be gained.

My work as a professional entertainer now ran in tandem with appearances on television and radio, where I was usually introduced as a 'White Witch'. And in 1971 Arnold and I presented the first series on witchcraft for B.B.C. Radio Sheffield entitled "*A Spell of Witchcraft*". I received invitations to give talks on witchcraft to many societies and clubs, and on several different occasions, at the University of Sheffield. There were engagements as an after-dinner speaker, and when my book, *Lid off the Cauldron* was first published in 1981, I was invited to appear on three radio stations in London. The first of these was for the B.B.C, Radio 4 programme, "*Start the Week*", presented at that time, by Richard Baker. The interviewer (or should I say, inquisitor!), was one Fred Housegoe, a London taxi-driver, who had achieved fame by winning "*Mastermind*" However, his attempts to introduce the usual approach of scepticism into the proceedings, failed miserably, and I held my own. Of the other guests on the programme, I knew only Mavis Nicholson, who had interviewed me in "*Afternoon Plus*", for Thames T.V.

Vicky, a friendly rep; from my publisher Frederick Muller, accompanied me round the city, and after lunch, it was time for Radio London, where I met Tony Blackburn. He was a great character, bubbling with enthusiasm and friendliness, and I thoroughly enjoyed talking to him. A female presenter interviewed me on Capital Radio, which turned out to be a most positive discussion on witchcraft. These appearances were closely followed by others, including Harlech T.V., for Wales and the West of England, and B.B.C. television's "*Look North*".

I received a letter from London Weekend Television to appear on a children's programme and discovered that the company had taken over the old Granville Theatre at Walham Green. I had often played there in the past and being in one of the original dressing-rooms, was a nostalgic experience. The auditorium had been torn out and transformed into a television studio, but at least the building still served the purpose of entertainment. I planned to tell the children about the Goddess, and how she could still be seen on our currency as Britannia, or Brigantia. The producer, Joy Whitby, thought it was a fine idea and enlargements of the now old penny, and the pound note, illustrated the commentary. Bernard Bresslaw who had a part in the programme was to interview me, but for some reason he was unable to form suitable questions, so Joy arranged for me to talk directly to camera.

With Arnold's help, I developed a children's show which featured magic, music, and string marionettes, and thoroughly enjoyed this new venture. Arnold had made over 500 puppets of various kinds over the years, he either carved them in wood, or created them from *papier-mache*, and each one was a real work of art.

One day while watching *"What's My Line?"* on television, I suddenly recognised Jean Carlin, a lady ventriloquist, as one of the acts from my very first summer show in Saltburn. This gave me the idea of taking part in the show, myself, and as the producer, Maurice Leonard, was someone whom I had met several times in the past, I wrote to him. My letter resulted in a successful interview in Leeds, and I was 'in Meredith!'.

My label on "*What's My Line?*" was Patricia Crowther - Puppeteer', and I had decided to use the skeleton. This marionette's legs, arms and head, separates from its torso, which looks very effective when it dances to the music.

I followed the guest celebrity's spot, when the panel don black-velvet masks and the said celebrity disguises his or her voice. While waiting in the wings, a tiny lady appeared out of the gloom, and enquired, "Is this the way on?" I affirmed that it was, and recognised Thora Hird. While Miss Hird was on, I asked one of the stage-hands to hold the controls of the skeleton until I came for it, and not to let go on pain of death!

The panel consisted of Jilly Cooper, the novelist, Garth Crookes (sportsman), Philip Schofield, the actor, and the impressionist, Faith Brown The presenter was Angela Rippon - delightful to work with, and a thoroughly nice person in every sense of the word. They were all extremely complimentary when they posed questions. Faith thought I looked like an entertainer and said she had noticed my stature and elegance! Allowed ten questions, the panel got me in six. While Angela explained that I had brought along one of my puppets, I retrieved it from the faithful stage-hand and waited for the music to start, but nothing happened! So, after a slight panicky pause, I walked on and worked the puppet in silence, with the exception of appreciative gasps of surprise and laughs from the panel and the studio audience. Working the marionette without the music, felt very strange and unreal, but being a professional artiste I knew I had to do it. When the programme was transmitted some months later, the music was included, and the skeleton danced to it, just as though it had done so in the recording, so that was fine by me. Obviously, the music had been played at the time, but they had forgotten to relay it into the studio. On the whole, *"What's My Line?"* made a refreshing change from other television programmes, where I appeared as a witch, and often had to face cynical or prejudiced minds.

I took part in the television panel game, *"Tell the Truth"*, and the most exciting part of the show for me was meeting Pat Reid, the author of *Escape from Colditz*, who was the subject of another recording of the panel game that day. Pat Reid escaped from the German prison camp, Colditz, during the second World War, a castle built upon a high rock where escape was considered to be well nigh impossible. Pat, along with several other prisoners, proved them wrong!

My work as an entertainer continued unabated, and dining a cabaret for the Sherwood Foresters, in Bakewell, Arnold and I were approached by Mr. Fisher, the then comptroller of Chatsworth House, in Derbyshire, and invited to present a show at their annual Christmas Party. Although this entertainment was mainly for the children, adults, including the Duke and Duchess of Devonshire, were also present. I did not know at the time that my services would be required at Chatsworth on other occasions in the future - two of them with Arnold, and after my husband passed over, presenting the show, myself.

I was thrilled to be booked for Chatsworth House, as I adore these stately homes which contain so many beautiful rooms and treasures, and all the history which lies behind them. And on each of *my* visits, at least, the itinerary for the Christmas Party followed a set pattern. You were requested to enter the grounds of the estate through the Golden Gates opened specially for you. Arriving at the House, attendants were on hand to carry your cases and apparatus through the celebrated Painted Hall, and thence, via the grand staircase, to the room in which the entertainment was to be held. I always admired a wonderful bronze statue of Mercury which stood at the top of the staircase.

The room, itself, was very long and had huge windows which looked onto the gardens and the park, beyond. Gold-painted chairs with red-velvet cushions were arranged in rows facing the platform erected for the show. The first time Arnold and I appeared there, the lighting was quite subdued but on our second visit, the Duchess, recognising this deficiency, had a spotlight placed on the wall so that the platform was properly lit - especially for the marionettes. Her Grace thought they were fascinating.

Tea was held in the Painted Hall, so called because of the exquisite ceiling depicting the Greek gods and goddesses in various legends. We were always invited to sit down for tea, but that took up the preparation time, as the show followed directly afterwards, so a tray was brought up for us.

32. A hug from actor Christopher Biggin after the recording of television's panel game "Tell the Truth". Photo Ian Lilleyman

When I performed the show, alone, I stepped onto the platform; glanced at the large oil painting of King Henry the Eighth on the wall behind me, and quipped, "I hope it is not that kind of platform!" which brought the first laugh of the show. Afterwards, the Duchess said how much they had enjoyed it. She was appreciative of the fact that there was never a moment without laughter, or audience participation, and commented, "I don't know *how* you do it!"

Later, I recalled an entertainments manager in Scotland, saying the same thing. I think the show is successful because I never dwell too long on a trick or effect, and switch from magic to puppets, and from music to rope-spinning, so the children don't lose interest, and are attentive throughout the performance. There is also the fact that I have a natural rapport with children and never talk down to them. In my natal astrological chart, the moon is situated in the sign of Gemini - the sign of the young, and of the 'young at heart', and therefore explains part of my character and personality.

The moon has always been primarily associated with the feminine aspects of life, as she governs the cycles of menstruation (mens, meaning moon), revolving round the Earth in about twenty-eight days - once a month, or moon. She also rules the seminal fluid, pearly-white, like the orb itself, and so influences both human and animal fertility. The moon controls the ebb and flow of the tides, which are highest when she is new or full, and of course, she has always been known as the 'Mistress of Magic'.

Witches work their beneficent magic when the moon is waxing or when it is full, using a waning moon for banishing adverse conditions in themselves, or in others. The moon has been a symbol of the Great Goddess since time immemorial, hence one of her epithets, 'Goddess of the Moon'.

All the planets and luminaries were named after the gods, who in turn, personified the great powers of Nature. Certainly, their influences are considered to manifest through the heavenly bodies in various ways and aspects; this being the basis of astrology. Initiates of most traditions understand that manifested Nature is force incarnating in form, and it is also understood that these forces are *not* blind but are of an intelligence much greater than that of humanity. And in order that men might draw closer to them, images and statues were created for these forces to ensoul and given the names of particular gods and goddesses. As one significant rubric of the Western Mystery Tradition informs us, "For by Names and Images are all Powers awakened and re-awakened."

The return of the Great Goddess had long been predicted, and although she had always been acknowledged within the confines of hereditary covens, and secret meetings of free-thinking pagans on moonlit nights in the woodlands, the time had arrived for the Goddess to be recognised on a world-wide scale. For too long, the patriarchal religions had ruled over people's minds, and subconsciously, many felt that something was missing. That 'something', was the Goddess, who embodies the feminine aspect of the Divine, and the whole of Womanhood.

The Horned God, also known as the 'Green Man', has always been the consort of the Great Goddess. He is the wild, untamed aspect of Nature and recognised by witches and pagans as the God of the Woodlands. To the Mediterranean peoples he was known as the Great God Pan, the masculine spirit of Nature - all pervading and all powerful.

Several years ago, in Graves Park, Sheffield, the sculptor Rod Powell carved an image of the 'Green Man' from a living tree. The god, with antlered head outlined against the sky, surveys his domain - a truly magical sight. And as the years progressed and the seasons changed, so the appearance of the carving changed, too, and today, lichen mottles his features and the ivy advances, as if it yearns to touch the eldest god and cover his limbs with its tenacious tendrils.

The name, the 'Green Man', is prevalent in Sheffield and in other towns and cities across Britain. Every time I approach a pedestrian crossing, the 'Green Man' tells me when it is safe to cross the road. At the top of Commercial Street, a warning sign reads: - CAUTION! CROSS ONLY WITH GREEN MAN.

Whoever created this type of crossing, was probably unaware of any connection between their invention and that of the ancient god. It is, however, a fortuitous coincidence that the 'Green Man', who in ancient times was thought of as a guardian and protector, has today (albeit in name only) been incorporated in a system designed to give the populace safe passage.

Stirrings of the renaissance of witchcraft had already begun when man fulfilled his oldest dream in travelling to the moon. I believe that amazing journey became the trigger, on the physical plane, which set in motion the magical current, already activated, for the return of the Goddess. By setting foot on the moon, man created a link with the Goddess, Herself.

The main thrust of the renaissance of the Old Religion came from the work and endeavours of Gerald Brosseau Gardner, who loved the Goddess. And when Gerald passed over to the Summerland in 1964 I automatically took over his task, and through the spoken and written word enlightened a mostly uninformed audience on the theology, ethics, and fundamental truths of this most ancient faith. Today, the Old Religion is described as the fastest-growing religion in the Western World, and in its new form as 'Wicca', is the only one which has sprung directly from the British Isles.

33. The 'Green Man' in Graves Park, Sheffield. Photo: Christine Koehldorfer

34. In the modern age, the Green Man - the ancient god - is still associated, albeit subconsciously, with protection and safe passage.
Photo: Ian Lilleyman

The Goddess calls not only to the female but also to the male. The mystical rituals and other-world atmosphere of the candle-lit Circle evoking the inner and opposite nature, which in a man is always feminine. It is this hidden self, in touch with beauty and its expression through poetry, music and art, which is seldom allowed to flourish in modern society. Therefore it is fitting for this work to contain a verse written by a late High Priest of the Craft and initiate of the Sheffield Coven, whose magical name was Hesus.

PRAYER TO THE GODDESS

"O heavenly mother, celestial womb,
Goddess of all the Gods in One,
Our earthly cradle and our tomb
From dawn of life to setting sun.
I praise Thee for Thy many blessings,
All the gifts of bounteous earth,
With the loveliness of living
Through each spiral of rebirth.
I thank Thee for my presence here,
The breath of life Thou gavest me,
And as Thy sun, reborn each year,
I serve Thee now, eternally."

Appendix
The Jean MacDonald Letters

The letters I received from the Scottish High Priestess, Jean MacDonald in 1962/3, were discussed in my autobiography "One Witch's World" (paperback "High Priestess"), and I have now decided to make some of them available for private viewing.

The correspondence from Jean is of tremendous importance because it confirms the validity and structure of the Craft as a continuous, unbroken tradition from the distant past. As Jean herself said, she came from a long line of witches as far back as the witch-hunting days. Hers was a family tradition.

There is an abundance of historical evidence associated with witches, and in Margaret Murray's distinguished work, "The Witch Cult of Western Europe" (Clarendon Press, Oxford 1921), under "Names of witches in covens", we find exactly that, including the towns and places they came from, and the years in which they were apprehended, banished, or executed. The list covers over 400 witches from the 15th to the 18th century.

However, apart from Gerald Gardner's own initiation into the Craft, Jean MacDonald's letters are perhaps the only other surviving link with the past, being written by an elderly witch towards the end of her life. They reveal that witchcraft rituals were being performed long before the time of Gardner. This is something that most adherents realise, but for too long there have been people who, for reasons of their own, assert that the Craft originated from Gerald Gardner and his works. Jean's letters and rites, however, are further evidence that it did not! And I firmly believe that like Jean's family, there must be many other 'witch families' where the knowledge is handed down through the centuries.

36. Patricia Crowther, in ceremonial dress, consecrates wine in the Horned Cup.
Photo: Gwion

www.ingramcontent.com/pod-product-compliance
Lightning Source LLC
Chambersburg PA
CBHW071621080526
44588CB00010B/1215